The
Research
Virtuoso

How to Find Anything You Need to Know

Fully
revised
and
updated

Art by
victoR gad

 annick press
toronto + new york + vancouver

Researched and written by Jessica Rovito and Peggy Thomas
Edited by Laura Edlund
Cover design by Sheryl Shapiro
Interior design by Kong Njo
Index card with paperclip on page 81, © iStockphoto Inc./Leo Blanchette.
Website template on page 36, © iStockphoto Inc./bubaone.

We acknowledge the support of the Canada Council for the Arts, the Ontario Arts Council, and the Government of Canada through the Canada Book Fund (CBF) for our publishing activities.

**ONTARIO ARTS COUNCIL
CONSEIL DES ARTS DE L'ONTARIO**

Cataloging in Publication

    The research virtuoso : how to find anything you need to know / Toronto Public Library ; art by victoR gad. — Fully rev. and updated ed.

First ed. published under title: The research virtuoso : brilliant methods for normal brains.
Includes bibliographical references and index.
Issued also in electronic formats.
ISBN 978-1-55451-394-9

    1. Internet searching—Handbooks, manuals, etc. 2. Electronic information resource searching—Handbooks, manuals, etc. 3. Library research—Handbooks, manuals, etc. I. Gad, Victor II. Toronto Public Library

ZA3075.R46 2012   001.4'2   C2011-907313-7

Distributed in Canada by:
Firefly Books Ltd.
66 Leek Crescent
Richmond Hill, ON
L4B 1H1

Published in the U.S.A. by Annick Press (U.S.) Ltd.
Distributed in the U.S.A. by:
Firefly Books (U.S.) Inc.
P.O. Box 1338
Ellicott Station
Buffalo, NY 14205

Printed in Canada

Visit us at: www.annickpress.com
Visit Toronto Public Library at:
    www.torontopubliclibrary.ca
Visit victoR gad at: www.victorgad.com

MIX
Paper from
responsible sources
FSC
www.fsc.org   FSC® C004071

Contents
ııııııııııııııııııııııııııııııı

Acknowledgments

|||||||||||||||||||||||||||||||||||||||||||||||||||||||||||||||

We've had a great time writing this research guide. Even though we had fancied ourselves to have achieved research virtuoso status, we were pleasantly surprised to learn many new things along the way; this only serves to underscore the fact that learning is a lifelong endeavor.

One of the most exciting aspects of this rewrite has been the convergence of our own personal journeys and experiences. Peggy's background in education helped drive the book's focus on process. For Jessica, this was the seed that shaped her writing and made this book different, painting a fuller picture of research as a meaningful activity.

There's nothing new about seeking information. What's changed is the flood of information that inundates our lives. Our hope is that the tools in this book will help you become critical consumers and navigators of information, creating your own meaning along the way.

Throughout this journey, we have encountered many people who have helped shape this book. Our thanks go out to our colleagues at Toronto Public Library: Anne Bailey, Linda Davis, Phyllis Malette, Ab Velasco, Gwyn Robson, Derek Eng, Joanne Bar, and Phyllis Jacklin. A special thanks goes out to the Downsview Branch of the Toronto Public Library for their flexibility and support. We'd also like to thank our friends at Annick Press: Katie Hearn, Chandra Wohleber, victoR gad, and Laura Edlund for their valuable advice and guidance.

On a personal note, many thanks to Jeremy Mulder for his inspiration, and to our families for their continual support.

— Jessica Rovito and Peggy Thomas

Foreword

Imagine signing out your own librarian—a knowledgeable guide who shows you how to find the best reliable information on the Internet, in the library, and beyond. Imagine a specialist who keeps in touch with the latest trends and resources, just so you can benefit from them. In *The Research Virtuoso*, Toronto Public Library brings you some of a librarian's expertise in a compact guide so you will be ready to face the often daunting prospect of conducting serious research in the information age.

In September 2005, *Research Ate My Brain*—the Toronto Public Library's research handbook for teens—was released in bookstores across North America. In 2006, when Annick Press approached the Library about collaborating on a follow-up book for older readers, it was a natural next step.

The guide is now fully revised and updated to include a wealth of new sources and an exploration of the *process* of researching. *The Research Virtuoso* covers conceiving, organizing, carrying out, and recording research for papers and projects. It goes on to show how effective research skills will help you succeed not only at school, but also in life.

In addition to consulting library users and staff, the Library gathered valuable input from instructors and librarians in academic institutions. The Library would like to thank Ab Velasco for his hard work in researching and writing the original manuscript, and Jessica Rovito and Peggy Thomas for their work on rewriting this latest edition.

With *The Research Virtuoso*, the librarian steps out from behind the reference desk and joins you in discovering exciting worlds of knowledge.

— Jane Pyper, City Librarian, Toronto Public Library

Introduction

It's not the destination but the journey that counts. So what does this old saying have to do with you? Don't worry, you didn't just pick up a self-help book by mistake—this *really* is a research guide. If you're reading this book in your hour of need, desperately seeking help with a research paper that's due tomorrow, then you're probably a little disappointed by that first sentence. But trust me: everything goes back to that old saying eventually. Yes, even your dreaded research assignment.

Learning *how* to research properly gives you a valuable skill for the rest of your life. Even if you never have to write another essay again, you'll continue to research one thing or another, most times without even realizing it. Your future research needs might include things like getting ready to buy a car, gathering information about

1

a potential employer, or deciding where to go on vacation. Consider buying a new mobile device for a moment. With all the choices available in contracts, data plans, and so on, things can get a bit overwhelming. To make an informed decision, you'll have to weigh all of your options. And believe it or not, this book will help you do just that. Or how about staying up-to-date on the latest musicians, movies, or trends? Well, that's a part-time job on its own, one that will undoubtedly benefit from your intimate knowledge of the research process.

This book shows you how to become a *research virtuoso*. The word *virtuoso* comes from the Latin word for *virtuous* and denotes someone with remarkable skill and integrity. What sets a research virtuoso apart from the average researcher is not only skill level but also the fact that the research virtuoso is excited about doing research. Although you might not see it now, with your assignment deadline looming, being *able* to do research is more than necessary and valuable—it's a privilege, and it's your chance to contribute to the creation of new knowledge.

It's easy to take the freedom to conduct research for granted. Using the words *research* and *freedom* in the same sentence might seem like an oxymoron, but these seemingly contradictory words actually form the core of what's called *academic freedom*. Academic freedom enables researchers to investigate unpopular and controversial topics without fear of getting in trouble. This type of independence is the cornerstone of academic communities—colleges and universities— around the world. Recognizing that you have the freedom to conduct research in the first place is a step along the road to becoming a research virtuoso.

Along with this freedom comes the responsibility to report your ideas and findings honestly and accurately. I'm talking about the big *P* here: *plagiarism*. Passing off someone else's work as your own can sometimes be an honest slipup, with your failure to acknowledge a source being nothing more than an innocent oversight. In these in-stances, poor planning and organizational skills are often the culprit.

The tips in this book will help you guard against plagiarism and give you the tools to uphold academic honesty. But wait . . . that's not all. This book will guide you in how to access source material effectively and efficiently. The ABCs of evaluating information will help you to become a critical consumer of information, and the checklists at the end of each section will help you to stay on top of what needs to get done. The Grab & Go pages are templates to use throughout your research process.

So what are you waiting for? Crack this book open and take pleasure in the journey because, before you know it, you'll have reached your destination and your research assignment will be pretty well mapped out. And you'll be on your way to reaching research virtuoso status!

Getting Ready: Preparing Yourself for Research

A Map for Digging Deeper

Whether you're preparing to go off to college or university or you're already there, you need to know that the expectations of a postsecondary environment are greater than what's expected of you in high school. With this in mind, you need to step up your academic game. Acquainting yourself with Bloom's Taxonomy can help you do just that.

In 1956, a famous educational psychologist named Benjamin Bloom wrote about the learning process as six different levels of achievement. The idea behind Bloom's Taxonomy—a structure that orders thinking skills into increasingly complex levels that build upon one another—is that critical thinking takes place at the higher levels. The taxonomy was slightly revised in the 1990s and continues to be used widely. Bloom's Taxonomy can be used as

- a framework to help you think about thinking and the research process in general
- a way to help you develop a focus for your research

Climbing the Ladder: Breaking Down Bloom

Higher-Order Thinking Skills

Evaluate and **create**—seen as the highest-level skills. The order of evaluate and create (synthesize) was changed in the 1990s revision of Bloom's Taxonomy. Creating (synthesizing) means creating a product that is uniquely yours, producing new meanings or structures. Evaluating can mean reflecting on that end product to assess its value or assessing the value of another expression—for example, what you analyzed in the previous level. Evaluating involves valuing, judging, arguing, defending, and so on.

Analyze—means that you can take ideas and information apart, examine them critically, look at their structure, compare, contrast, and so on.

Apply—means taking the learning further by applying the learning in a real-life situation, demonstrating it, sketching it, and so on.

Understand—means that you comprehend facts and ideas; you understand their meaning in order to paraphrase or explain them, and so on.

Remember—means that you can recall facts and ideas from memory and can list them.

Lower-Order Thinking Skills

Why Scratch When You Can Dig?

Research virtuosos dig deep into their subjects. In contrast, students who don't push themselves beyond the lower-order thinking skills of remembering and understanding merely scratch the surface of a subject. Postsecondary education challenges you to move beyond simple understanding and encourages you to develop strong critical thinking skills, nudging you along the scale of Bloom's Taxonomy as you go.

The key steps that follow will help you dig deeper in this stage of the research process. At the end of this section, we'll take a look at how checking Bloom's Taxonomy can help you make sure you are digging deep enough into your research assignment.

First Step: Make Friends with Your Research Assignment

Believe it or not, your assignment sheet is a treasure trove of information!

Understand what's being asked of you: The University of North Carolina at Chapel Hill (UNC-CH) Writing Center recommends (and we agree!): read your assignment carefully as soon as you receive it, and ask for clarification about anything you don't understand. Consider the types of words used on the assignment sheet. Some common key words and their definitions are listed below.

- **Define:** Give the subject's meaning.
- **Explain:** Give reasons or examples of why something happened.
- **Compare:** Present similarities.
- **Contrast:** Present differences.
- **Assess:** Summarize how your subject measures up to a set of preestablished criteria—either your own criteria established for this purpose or those of an expert.
- **Analyze:** Break down the topic into its parts to understand the parts, how the parts relate to one another, what the topic means, and how it works.
- **Argue:** State a thesis or choose a side, and defend your position with arguments that support your view and dispute other views.

There are different types of research papers and essays, so make sure you understand which one you are expected to write. Here are some of the more popular types and examples for a single subject:

Types	Examples
Cause and effect	• What effect has the U.S. Supreme Court's landmark *Roe v. Wade* decision had on the abortion debate in America?
Compare and contrast	• Compare and contrast the American and Canadian legal precedent(s) on abortion.
Survey of current thinking	• Summarize the current public debate over abortion.
Position paper	• Do you believe that abortion should be legal? Explain your position and provide support.

Research Paper or _____? Be Creative if You Can Swing It

Although the most–used means of disseminating research is a research paper, it's not the only game in town. Your assignment might allow for—or require—a different way of communicating your results. But before you settle on a particular format, remember to check the requirements of the assignment and even double-check with the person who assigned it.

This book will help guide you along the research process no matter what format of communication you use. And in Section 4, you'll find useful tips on putting together a presentation, as well as ideas about how to present your research in other formats.

Discipline-Specific Writing

As you move further along in your postsecondary pursuits, you will be expected to specialize in one particular discipline. The research tasks faced by students in different disciplines can be vastly different, and each area of study comes with its own set of expectations. Take academic studies in English literature and history, for example:

- As an **English literature student**, you might be asked to critically evaluate two literary works and provide support from scholarly publications. In this case, your essay should attempt to persuade the reader that your perspective on those literary works is valid.
- As a **history student**, you might be asked to compare primary documents on a historical movement (with particular emphasis on one key figure) to historians' interpretation of these events as found in secondary sources.

Make sure you familiarize yourself with the expectations of your chosen discipline and clarify your assignment requirements.

Set Up a Research Plan

Developing a research plan will help to keep you focused throughout the research process and as you draft, revise, and finalize your results. Here are some tips:

1. **Understand the research process:** The time line illustration below is like a map for the journey ahead. However, here are some cautions:

   - Some parts of the research process (such as locating and processing information) take more time than others, so make sure you plan for this.

- The research process is rarely lockstep and linear. You will often find that stages in the process overlap. Also, you will find yourself moving back and forth between stages.

A research virtuoso establishes a time line for every project. The sections of this book loosely follow the time line laid out below.

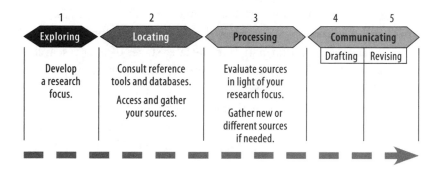

2. **Create a schedule:** Jot down all the things you need to do, along with deadlines for each, in an agenda or online calendar. Commit to specific days and times for completing the different stages of research.
3. **Use checklists:** You will find a Get Organized Checklist at the end of each section, in the Grab & Go pages. These checklists will help you stay on top of what needs to get done along the way.

Gather Your Thoughts

Like their hunter-gatherer counterparts, researchers have to both hunt (for specific pieces of information) and gather (their thoughts, that is). The end product may not be appetizing, but it sure as heck is satisfying.

When starting any research process, it's important to take the time to gather up your ideas and existing knowledge on the topic— in other words, brainstorm. This brainstorming stage will help you move on later to hunt for more information.

- **Make a list:** Jot down what you already know about the topic and what kinds of information you still need.
- **Make it personal:** Think about how the topic relates to your life and your personal interests, and try to connect those to your topic.
- **Make a bank of key words:** Start to compile a list of words and synonyms related to your topic.
  - ▸ Use the template Key Word Bank (Grab & Go page 25). A big bank of key words will help you search for appropriate information in the later stages of your research.
  - ▸ Add to your Key Word Bank on an ongoing basis as you come across new terms.
- **Make a map:** Concept mapping can generate different ways of thinking about a topic. A visual organizer will help you classify and extend your ideas by mapping them according to larger concepts.
  - ▸ You could use the template Topic Brainstorm Web (Grab & Go page 26) to get started.
  - ▸ If you are working on an assignment that will involve comparing and contrasting, you could use the template Venn Diagram (Grab & Go page 27) to get started. The sample on page 13 shows how a Venn diagram can help you brainstorm and organize your ideas.
  - ▸ Consider using concept mapping software to extend your ideas:
    - ▹ **Visual Understanding Environment (VUE)**—an open source project based at Tufts University
    - ▹ **bubbl.us**—a free Web-based application that lets you brainstorm online
    - ▹ **Cmap Tools**—a free concept-mapping tool from the Institute for Human and Machine Cognition (IHMC)
    - ▹ **SMART Ideas**—fee-based concept-mapping software

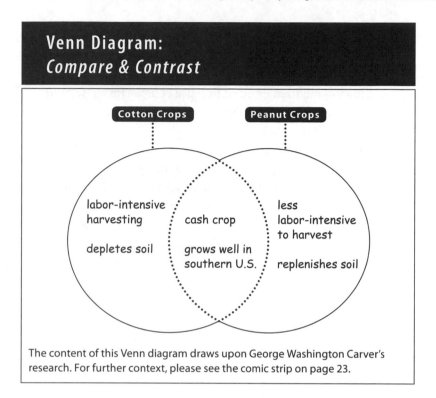

Venn Diagram: *Compare & Contrast*

Cotton Crops   **Peanut Crops**

labor-intensive harvesting

depletes soil

cash crop

grows well in southern U.S.

less labor-intensive to harvest

replenishes soil

The content of this Venn diagram draws upon George Washington Carver's research. For further context, please see the comic strip on page 23.

Pick Some Brains: Not Just for Zombies

When starting the research process, it's easy to forget about the people right in front of you. Take the time to tap into the knowledge and expertise of others by picking the brains of your professors, instructors, teachers, TAs (teaching assistants), and librarians. To make the best use of their time and yours, you may want to do this only *after* you have carefully read the assignment and gathered your current knowledge and initial thoughts.

- **Faculty:** Schedule a meeting with your professor, instructor, teacher, or TA. Ask any clarifying questions you have about the assignment and about the faculty member's perspective on the topic.

- At most colleges and universities, teaching staff have regularly scheduled office hours—specific times when they open their offices to students and their questions. Often this is a job requirement, and because you pay for these hours through your tuition fees, you should definitely make good use of all they can offer!

- **Librarians:** It's a librarian's job to help you articulate your information needs, and at this stage of the game, that's exactly what you should be doing! Consider visiting your local public, general academic, or special subject library for the expertise librarians can offer. You might be able to book an appointment with a librarian for help with the research process. Some librarians even take questions over the phone, via online chat services, and by e-mail.

  - Many university and college libraries, as well as large public library systems, hire librarians with expertise in a particular area. Talking to these specialized librarians is something to consider at all stages of your research.

General Reference Sources: A Researcher's First Date

The first look at sources for a research assignment can be kind of like a first date: it can be awkward, but it's an introduction and gives you a better understanding of what's ahead. Once you've finished brainstorming, make a first date with some general reference sources. The information in these resources will help you get an overview of the subject and will prepare you to research your topic further. These resources can be found either in print or online. Pay close attention to the publication dates because how up-to-date they are is often their greatest asset.

General References by Category	Examples
Dictionaries—sources that go beyond simply defining words. Thematic dictionaries are handy for defining a subject's concepts and terminology.	• *Newton's Telecom Dictionary: Telecommunications, Networking, Information Technologies, The Internet, Wired, Wireless, Satellites and Fiber* is useful for gaining a better understanding of the Internet and telecommunications and to keep up-to-date on rapidly changing technologies. • The wide range of Oxford dictionaries is available online via subscription. • *Elsevier's Dictionary of Eponyms* can help you learn about real-life people who have become immortalized in the English language.
Encyclopedias—books or sets of books that relay general information on many topics, which are arranged in alphabetical order.	• *The Oxford Encyclopedia of Women in World History* contains information about women from all fields and disciplines of study.

(Continued)

General References by Category	Examples
Atlases—resources containing maps, charts, and other visuals. Atlases relay specific facts by region, theme (e.g., politics, environment), and so on.	• historical atlases—e.g., *Mapping Epidemics: A Historical Atlas of Disease* • cultural atlases—e.g., *Wayland Atlas of Threatened Cultures* • thematic atlases—e.g., *The Penguin Atlas of Endangered Species*
Gazetteers—dictionaries of geographic identifiers, which can be either text-based or numerical. These resources are available in print and online and are developing into very complex tools.	• *The Columbia Gazetteer of the World* is a multivolume set with an online version (available by subscription only). • Geographic Names Information System (GNIS) is a free online resource of the U.S. government, with multiple maps coordinated within the gazetteer.
Textbooks, handbooks, manuals—general books on a subject and resources frequently used in the sciences as quick reference sources. These sources are often good starting points and may contain statistical information. Course materials often identify these types of sources specific to an area of study.	• *The Merck Manual of Diagnosis and Therapy* (usually referred to as simply *The Merck Manual*) is a popular medical textbook.
Almanacs—annual publications containing useful and current statistics and other facts	• The *Farmer's Almanac* is a well-known resource for long-range weather predictions. • The *Canadian Almanac & Directory* is a resource that offers a comprehensive picture of the Canadian economic, business, political, social, and geographic reality.

General References by Category	Examples
Biographical resources—compilations of concise biographical information on a specific group of people	• *Marquis Who's Who* gives comprehensive biographical data about the lives of today's leaders, from the United States and around the world, in every significant field of endeavor. • *Canadian Who's Who* lists biographical information on prominent living Canadians.
Directories—resources that help you to look up names, phone numbers, or addresses. Directories come in handy when looking for experts in a particular field.	• Scott's Business Directories Online is a subscription-based compilation of Canadian company information by product, type, location, exports, demographics, and contact information.
Bibliographies—lists of works on a particular subject or by a particular author. Some bibliographies are annotated, summarizing the most current books and articles on a particular subject; these can be very helpful.	• *The Spanish-American War and Philippine Insurrection, 1898–1902: An Annotated Bibliography* lists and summarizes various works about the war. • The *Bibliography of Canadian Bibliographies* is an entire book of lists of published bibliographies on various topics related to Canadian history, culture, politics, etc.

Reference Management Tools: Tracking Your Trawling

As you research, you will find many interesting and relevant sources, but keeping track of them requires some planning. A great way to track sources is to use reference management software. Online research management tools such as those listed below let you create a personal database of references by importing and organizing citations (written references to specific works) from research databases, library catalogs, and even Google Scholar. These tools can format your bibliography for you, so you can create one in no time at all.

- RefWorks (available by subscription)
- BibDesk (free software for Mac users)
- BibMe (free, Web-based)
- EndNote (available by subscription)
- Zotero (free; requires a specific browser)

Most colleges and universities pay for mass subscriptions to RefWorks or other research management products, which means you'll get them for free!

Avoid the Data Deluge

One of the greatest things—as well as one of the most challenging—about digital information is that it's so readily available and easy to produce.

- According to an article in *The Chronicle of Higher Education*, Johns Hopkins University researchers working on the Sloan Digital Sky Survey acquired more data about astronomy in their first two days on the project, in 2000, than the entire history of humanity had previously acquired on the subject!
- According to *The Economist*, in 2005, humanity created 150 exabytes of data according to one estimate. In 2010, it was predicted that humanity would create 1,200 exabytes of data. (One exabyte equals 1 billion gigabytes.)

While you do your research, it's important to find a reasonable—but not overwhelming—amount of information. If you rush straight from getting your assignment into grabbing anything and everything that might relate to your topic, you'll end up creating a deluge of data with all kinds of unrelated information. One way to guard against data overload is to spend some time up front developing a research focus. Section 2 also helps you figure out when you have enough and can stop looking for information. See page 29.

Target a Research Focus

You'll finish your assignment sooner and more efficiently if you develop a research focus early on. Having a focus will help you steer clear of time-wasters such as unrelated information.

Once you've taken some time to gather your own background knowledge, seek out the knowledge of others, and consult some general reference sources, review what you have and where you are going with the following questions:

- **What am I studying/working on?**
- **What *exactly* do I want to find out?**
- **What do I want my audience to understand?**

If your professor (or instructor, teacher, etc.) assigns an essay on the topic of communications scholar Marshall McLuhan, for example, you might begin to satisfy these questions through the following research focus:

I am researching **social media through the lens of McLuhan's famous statement "the medium is the message"** because I want to find out **if user-generated content is capable of creating new forms of community**. I would like to help my audience understand that, **when the media environment changes, human relations change too.**

To help define a research focus, remember to refer to

- any notes you've made about addressing all assignment requirements
- your brainstorming ideas (see Topic Brainstorm Web, Grab & Go page 26)

All that work you did to generate new ideas and subtopics will help you to form a more focused area for exploration. Take the time to examine all of the different ideas you came up with by asking yourself the following questions:

- Are there any unusual ideas that don't seem to connect?
- Could some ideas be regrouped to form interesting juxtapositions?
- What exciting topics could come from the collision of these ideas?
- How could this lead to new, innovative, and original focus statements?

Don't Be Rude: Address Your Audience

So who exactly is your audience anyway, and why does this matter? Are you addressing a group or an individual who already shares your opinions about the subject, or one with a limited knowledge or understanding of the subject?

Knowing the audience you're writing for or presenting to will help you determine

- what material to include in your final product
- how to organize your ideas
- how best to support your argument, thesis, or position

As the University of North Carolina at Chapel Hill Writing Center notes, most of the time your audience will be the person who assigned the research task—for example, the professor who already knows everything about Marshall McLuhan—but this person still needs to assess *your* understanding of and thinking about the topic. Here's an easy rule to follow: strive to use clear, plain language to indicate your knowledge, comprehension, application, analysis, and synthesis of the material.

Don't Forget!

Before you go any further, make sure your research focus and choice of final product is targeted to your audience and the expectations of the assignment.

- The type of essay you're working on will, in part, be determined by the audience.
- The key words in your assignment sheet will give you clues about what it is your professor (or instructor, etc.) is really looking for.

Back to Bloom

As this section comes to a close, keep in mind Bloom's Taxonomy— it's your friend! You can use the six categories of learning and skills to begin to think deeply about your research topic and direct your future efforts. Drill deeper by using Bloom as a framework to move from simple to complex questions and ideas, and don't be afraid to come back to it at later stages of the research process. The template Digging Deeper with Bloom's Taxonomy (Grab & Go page 28) can help with this.

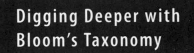

Digging Deeper with Bloom's Taxonomy

Here is an example of how to use the template on page 28.

Higher-Order Thinking Skills

Evaluate and Create—When the media environment changes, human relations change along with it.

Analyze—Can user-generated content create new forms of community?

Apply—This statement applies to today's social media.

Understand—The media through which we receive the information affects the way in which we perceive that information.

Remember—McLuhan posits that the medium is the message.

Lower-Order Thinking Skills

Evaluate and Create

Analyze

Apply

Understand

Remember

Get Organized Checklist:
Getting Ready

GRAB & GO

- ☐ I understand Bloom's Taxonomy and will use it as a guide to dig deeper into my research in order to analyze, evaluate, and create.

- ☐ I have carefully checked the research assignment and other expectations to understand the assignment requirements.

- ☐ I understand the research process and have committed myself to a research plan.

- ☐ I have gathered my existing knowledge and ideas.

- ☐ I have developed a list of key words and synonyms to use when searching for information.

- ☐ I have developed my ideas using maps or other visual organizers.

- ☐ I have accessed the knowledge of others, including teachers and librarians.

- ☐ I have consulted some general reference sources.

- ☐ I have investigated the reference management tools available to me.

- ☐ I have developed a focus for my research.

- ☐ I have considered my audience.

Key Word Bank

A research virtuoso does not rely on a single term or viewpoint to drive the research forward. A virtuoso builds a bank of related words and concepts to strengthen the search for information and access a deeper and broader pool of sources.

Look at **synonyms,** a **database thesaurus, subject headings, indexes, library catalogs,** and **abstracts** to generate a list.

Concept	Related Key Words
	<ul><li></li><li></li><li></li><li></li></ul>
	<ul><li></li><li></li><li></li><li></li></ul>
	<ul><li></li><li></li><li></li><li></li></ul>
	<ul><li></li><li></li><li></li><li></li></ul>

Topic Brainstorm Web

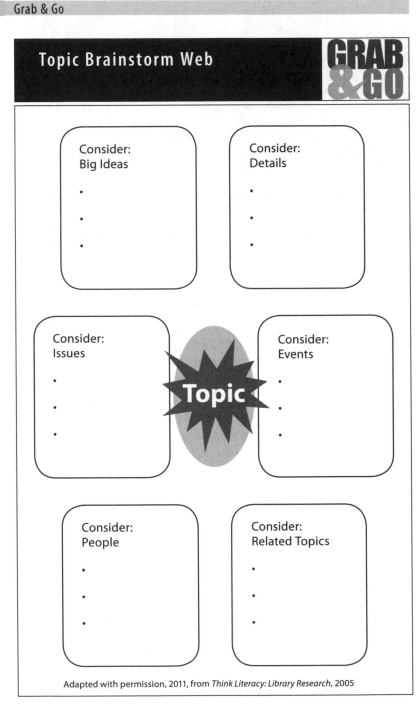

Consider:
Big Ideas

-
-
-

Consider:
Details

-
-
-

Consider:
Issues

-
-
-

Topic

Consider:
Events

-
-
-

Consider:
People

-
-
-

Consider:
Related Topics

-
-
-

Adapted with permission, 2011, from *Think Literacy: Library Research*, 2005

Venn Diagram:
Compare & Contrast

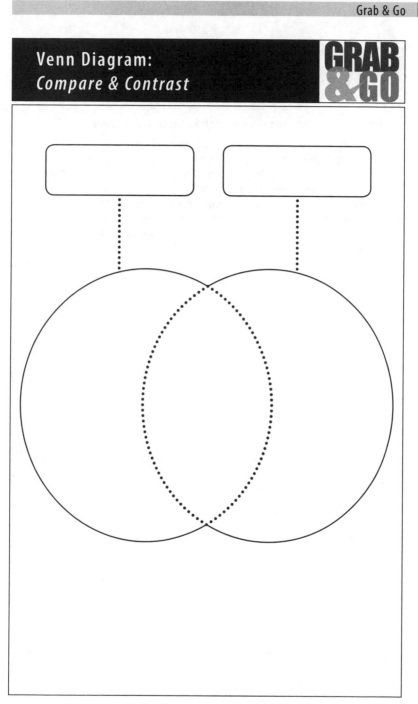

Digging Deeper with Bloom's Taxonomy

Use this chart to create a research focus that digs deeper.

1. Once you have a research focus drafted, examine it to see what thinking it involves and how you could place the research focus on the chart below. For example, will the focus make you remember and recall? connect facts? compare? create an alternative approach? Write it on the chart.

2. How could you revise or add to your research focus using the higher-order thinking skills? Space has been provided below to allow you to jot down your ideas.

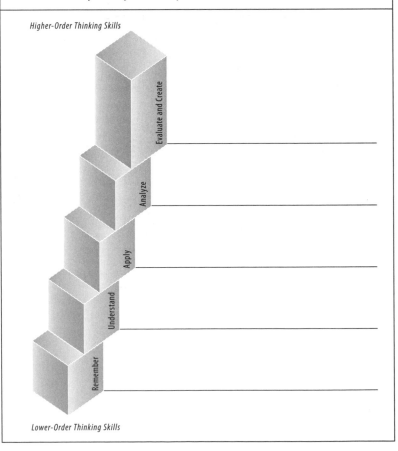

Higher-Order Thinking Skills

Evaluate and Create

Analyze

Apply

Understand

Remember

Lower-Order Thinking Skills

Digging In:
Locating Information

Now's the time to locate, select, and gather the most appropriate resources for your research. This section will teach you how to effectively locate information on the Internet, in the library, and at an archive, as well as how to tap into the knowledge of the people around you.

During this stage of locating information, if you think you need to reconsider your research focus or check in with your professor or instructor about your assignment, now's a great time to circle back. Remember: the research process isn't a one-way street!

Enough Already!
Know When to Stop Looking

As a research virtuoso, you know about the data deluge (page 18) and should know when to say, "Enough is enough!" As you work through the research process, keep the following in mind to evaluate whether to continue looking for additional sources or not:

- Do I have enough sources? (If this information doesn't appear on your assignment sheet, ask your professor, instructor, etc., for a guideline on how many sources to use. You can also ask at your school's writing center about the appropriate number of sources.)

(Continued)

- Do my sources explore the subject in enough depth?
- Do my sources include the key thinkers on the subject?
- Have I included sources that present current perspectives on the subject?
- Am I missing any leading thinkers, theories, or perspectives on my topic?
- Are my sources balanced in terms of perspectives? (Think about perspective and bias; refer to the section on the ABCs of evaluating sources for more information.)
- As a group, do my sources help me move beyond remembering or explaining to applying, analyzing, and evaluating?

The Three Types of Information

Deciding where to look for information will depend in part on what kinds of information you need. There are three main categories of information sources:

Primary Sources	First-hand accounts and observations created within the time frame being investigated. Some examples of primary sources include • letters • diaries or journals • blogs • government records • newspapers • artifacts • photographs (not manipulated) • interviews • police records and court documents • advertisements

Secondary Sources	Sources that restate, explain, or analyze a primary source. Secondary sources include • most books • dictionaries • articles • websites
Tertiary Sources	Books or articles that report on secondary sources. Some examples include • bibliographies • textbooks • encyclopedia articles

The Internet: A Great First Step

There once was a time when students were discouraged from using the Internet for any sort of research at all. Although this is no longer the case, you still need to be wary of what you find on the World Wide Web. Just about anyone can write something and put it online. Section 3 will show you how to evaluate information from the Internet (page 69), but for now, let's stick to the basics.

Contrary to popular belief, information is not always faster to find on the Internet. It depends on the kind of research you're doing; sometimes it's faster to look things up in a book or a general reference resource. The Internet is, however, a good place to start and an appropriate place to search for news and current information.

Nowadays researchers of all stripes use the Internet to access library resources, online databases, and even primary texts from reputable newspapers, journals, and other online sources. But the Internet isn't the only place they search. To become a research virtuoso, you need to consider a variety of resources, including print, electronic, and human.

Search Engines:
The Creepy Crawlers of the Information Universe

A search engine is a software program designed to help you find information on the World Wide Web. The engine matches the words you enter into its search box with different pages on the Internet. These programs are called *spiders*, and they crawl the Web by following one link to another—creepy indeed!

When a search engine points you to a website, it only knows that many others have looked at that same site; it does not consider the quality of the site's content. This is a crucial difference between search engines and other resources, such as subscription databases and books, in which humans have selected information based on specific criteria. Some general criteria can be found in Section 3's focus on the ABCs of evaluating sources (see page 68).

The Internet is full of different types of search engines, but at their core these tools include the same components:

- a search box in which you type your query
- a list of results

Google is the world's most popular search engine and is often the first place people turn to in order to search for information.

How to Be a Super Searcher

Search Well
Here are some things to keep in mind when using Web search engines:

- **Lowercase:** Search engines are not case-sensitive, so feel free to use lowercase letters only. For example, searching for *marshall mcluhan* will give the same results as searching for *Marshall McLuhan*.
- **Language:** Try to use the language that you think would most likely appear on the sorts of websites you're looking for. Refer back to the list of key words you compiled when you first began your research, and consider their synonyms (see Key Word Bank, page 25). For example, if you're doing research for a chemistry paper, searching for *fire retardant* will lead you to more technical sites than might a search for *fireproof*.

Search Widely

Using only one search engine will limit your results, so strive to be a super searcher by using different search engines. Different search engines produce different results because each uses a different algorithm to get the job done. In addition to competing search engine companies such as Google, Yahoo!, and Bing, there are different types of search engines developed by the same companies.

Take Google, for example. Google started out as a single Web search engine but now produces different types of search engines to meet different needs. For example

- **Google Images** allows you to search for images on the Web.
- **Google News** allows you to search thousands of online news stories.
- **Google Scholar** allows you to search for scholarly papers.

You can also search Google by using country-specific domain extensions. For example, Google.ca is for Canada and Google.co.uk is for the United Kingdom. See page 38 for more examples.

Join the Federation: Use a Metasearch Engine

When you use a *metasearch engine,* your query is automatically distributed to a bunch of search engines at once. These online resources perform what are called *federated searches,* facilitating simultaneous searches of the resources participating in the federation.

For example, the metasearch engine called Dogpile fetches results from Google, Yahoo!, Bing, Ask.com, and other popular search engines. Then it displays these results according to relevance, eliminating duplicate pages. As you'll find out on page 58, metasearch engines are particularly handy when searching for archival collections.

Constructing a Search Query

A *query* is simply the combination of words you enter into a search box. Some queries are more complex than others.

Check out the template Creating an Effective Search String (Grab & Go page 63). It can help you create an effective search query—one that uses advanced search features.

Searcher's Tricks of the Trade

Following are some tricks of the trade for conducting effective searches with Web search engines. Not all of these techniques will work in every search engine; to see which ones will and which ones won't, visit your chosen engine's help page, tips section, or support page. Take a look around to identify the search engine's features and how it compares with other search engines you know.

Maybe you use simple searches to find what you want most of the time. However, you likely get a lot of *hits* (search results) every time you do that. By including special characters or words (called *operators*) in your search, you give the search engine more precise instructions on how you want it to search. In the end, more precise instructions deliver more precise results.

The operators you'll learn about next are usually built into the advanced search options of search engines. You can use specialized search queries in what's called a simple search (the home page of any search engine) and get the same results as you would using an advanced search feature.

Searching a phrase: If you need to find either a proper name or an exact phrase, use quotation marks.

- For example, use quotation marks around this phrase from U.S. civil rights leader Rosa Parks to get results for the exact quotation: "The only tired I was, was tired of giving in."

Combining key words: There are a number of ways to combine key words to get more accurate search results. The most popular are listed below. You can use the template Creating an Effective Search String (Grab & Go page 63) to help.

- **Boolean searching**—Boolean searches combine the key words you want with the words *and, or,* or *not.* Some search engines require you to capitalize these words, but others don't; check the search engine's tips page to confirm.
  - ▶ **AND**—Use this operator when you want the engine to search for both terms. This is a popular operator to use when you want to narrow your search results.
    - ▷ For example, search for *marshall mcluhan* AND *university of toronto* if you want to retrieve pages that mention McLuhan's relationship with that university.
  - ▶ **OR**—Use this operator when you want the engine to search for a number of similar terms. The OR operator expands your search to retrieve a broader set of results.
    - ▷ For example, searching *for Aboriginal peoples OR First Nations OR Native Americans OR Indigenous peoples* will retrieve pages that use at least one of these terms.
  - ▶ **NOT**—Use this operator to exclude certain words from your search.
    - ▷ For example, if you search for *tree NOT evergreen,* you will exclude results containing information on evergreen trees.
- **Word math**—If you don't like Boolean searching, then word math might be your cup of tea. But remember: don't put a space between the mathematical symbol and your chosen search terms.
  - ▶ **Addition**—Use this operator to combine and include certain terms in your search.
    - ▷ For example, if you want to view pages about eagles and birds of prey generally, you may want to search for *eagles+raptors.*
  - ▶ **Subtraction**—Use this operator to exclude certain terms from your search.
    - ▷ For example, if you're researching eagles but don't want to view pages about the famous rock band the Eagles, you might search for *eagles–music.*

Searching within a website: By using the convention *site:xyz. com* (with no spaces in between), you can direct the search engine to narrow the search to within a single website.

> ▷ For example, if you want to search only the Smithsonian Institution's website (www.si.edu) for information on Amelia Earhart, enter the following in the search box: *site:www.si.edu Amelia Earhart*

URL Clues: What's in a Name?

The final part of a website's address can tell you something about who's providing the site's information. This part, called the domain extension, relays information about the site's host. Certain domain extensions are reserved for particular types of websites. Here are some common domain extensions:

.com	used by commercial companies
.org	used by nonprofit organizations
.net	used by Internet companies
.gov	used by U.S. government websites. Although other countries' government websites, including Canada's, might use the .gov extension somewhere in their address, they usually end in what's called a country code.
.ca	an example of a country code for Canada. Other codes include: .au (for Australia) .cn (for China) .ru (for Russia) .fr (for France)
.edu	used by American universities and other educational institutions. In contrast, most Canadian universities use .ca.

The Deep Web

The deep Web is the portion of the World Wide Web that conventional search engines cannot access. This harder-to-access part of the Web includes the content that lives in searchable databases. But don't let that get you down! Here are some examples of specialized search engines that will search this mysterious part of the Web for you:

Complete Planet	allows you to find databases with highly topical information in particular categories
Google Scholar	allows you to search a variety of academic databases for scholarly literature

Subject Directories: Humans Take Back Control

Web search engines are used to *explore* the World Wide Web, while *subject directories* are used when you want the exploring done for you. Sometimes called *subject guides* or *search directories*, subject directory websites are organized by people rather than by software. An advantage of using a subject directory is that the sites it lists are usually exclusively high-quality sites because someone has taken the time to evaluate them and has found them worthy of being included.

Subject directories are organized by categories and often have built-in search engines that allow you to search their collections of websites. Here are some examples of online subject directories:

ipl2	a merger of the former Internet Public Library (IPL) and the Librarians' Internet Index (LII) websites
Toronto Public Library's Virtual Reference Library (VRL)	access to librarian-selected websites as well as self-guided research support
INFOMINE Scholarly Internet Resource Collections	a list of websites maintained by the University of California, Riverside
Canadian Information By Subject	developed by Library and Archives Canada; provides links to information about Canada from Internet resources around the world

The Library: A Gateway to Information

Dismiss any thoughts of a search starting and ending with an Internet search engine. A whole other world of information is waiting for you and accessible through the library. The library is a great place to access primary, secondary, and tertiary sources.

Now let's get something straight: no two libraries are exactly the same. While most libraries are set up in a predictable fashion, each has its own unique collection of

- electronic resources
- periodicals (regular publications, including newspapers, magazines, and journals)
- books

As a result, take some time to orient yourself to *both*

- the library building (the bricks-and-mortar site, where the books are shelved, where you can go to ask for help face-to-face, etc.)
- the library website (how to access the catalog, where to get help online, etc.)

Library Websites: Gems of Online Research

Library websites are great resources in and of themselves. And don't forget: you can visit a library's website even if it's a library

- for which you don't have a card
- in a city you're just visiting
- for another college or university that's not your own

So what exactly can these online spaces offer? Well, besides the library's online catalog and database access, most academic library websites also include these wonders:

Guides authored by librarians: Academic libraries hire liaison or subject specialist librarians who have expertise in a particular discipline. It's part of their job to compile the following:

- **Subject guides**—recommended resources and tips for researching particular topics
- **Course guides**—like subject guides, but providing general research tips and listing recommended resources for certain courses

Online reference: If you enjoy chatting with your friends online, you'll love the ease of the virtual reference process. From your library's website, you can access a real-time chat research service to get one-on-one assistance from experienced staff in public and academic libraries.

Digital collections: There are some great digital library collections out there. Although some are housed in special databases or are available through database subscriptions only, a number of great resources are freely accessible online. For example:

- Duke University makes available historic photographs, advertisements, texts, and more from its unique library collections. *Emergence of Advertising in America: 1850–1920* (EAA) is an example of a subset of this collection. The EAA presents over 9,000 images and corresponding information related to the early history of advertising in the United States.
- The City of Toronto Archives has a searchable database of photographs.

OPAC: The Library Catalog That Never Sleeps

You don't necessarily need to be *in* a library building to search its catalog. Library catalogs are also accessible from a remote computer. Simply head over to a library's website to begin searching its online public access catalog (OPAC).

Take a few minutes to familiarize yourself with the OPAC's subject headings and the library's classification system. Here's where a librarian comes in handy. Librarians can easily translate your information needs into the precise subject headings used by the catalog, as well as into the library's overall classification structure—in other words, what call number system is used and which might be most helpful for you. Librarians speak OPAC!

OPACs also allow you to search by author, title, subject, or key word. These options are available either through a drop-down menu next to the catalog's search box or via an advanced search option.

Unless you instruct it not to, the library's catalog will likely simultaneously search all of the branches in the library system. So, if you want to search one specific library branch at a time, limit your search to that particular collection.

Calling All Call Numbers: Dewey versus Library of Congress

Libraries classify, organize, and shelve their materials by call numbers. Every book in a library has its own unique call number so it can easily be found on the shelf, and each set of library shelves is labeled with a range of call numbers. These are the two main classification systems used in North America:

- **Dewey Decimal System (DDC):** used by most public libraries. In this system, the different branches of knowledge are divided into 10 main categories, each indicated by the first digit in the Dewey Decimal System call number. The second and third digits in the call number further divide each category. DDC call numbers are often followed by a decimal point and an additional set of numbers that further narrow the subject area.

000	general works	500	pure science
100	philosophy	600	technology
200	religion	700	fine arts
300	social sciences	800	literature
400	language	900	history

- **Library of Congress System (LC):** used by most academic libraries. This system divides all branches of knowledge into 21 main categories, which are designated by letters of the alphabet.

A	general works	D	world history and history of Europe, Asia, Afric, Australia, New Zealand, etc.
B	philosophy, psychology, and religion		
C	auxiliary sciences of history—history of civilization, archaeology, genealogy, biography, etc.	E–F	history of the Americas
		G	geography, anthropology, recreation
		H	social sciences

J	political science		R	medicine
K	law		S	agriculture
L	education		T	technology
M	music		U	military science
N	fine arts		V	naval science
P	language and literature		Z	bibliography and library science
Q	science			

Without further ado, we present the reigning champions of library classification, LC and DDC, in a head-to-head competition of call numbers:

Breakdown of a Catalog Record

The library catalog helps you not only find a resource but also figure out whether a particular resource is relevant to your research. Each item in a library has a corresponding catalog record, and all catalog records are searchable through the OPAC.

Common Components of a Catalog Record

Call number and/or **location:** This tells you where in the library you can find the item. Library materials with similar content are given the same call number. When you arrive in the shelves or stack aisle to retrieve a book with a particular call number on it, you'll discover that the other books around it deal with a similar topic. For later reference in your research, you might want to compile a list of the call numbers you encounter for relevant books.

Not all call numbers are straightforward (and it's not uncommon for the same book to have different call numbers in different libraries). In a library system with more than one building, branch, or collection, a location code may be tacked onto the end of a call number. When in doubt, ask a librarian.

Additional special locations for library material might include these:

- **Course reserves** or **short-term loan**—Usually consisting of required and supplementary readings for a course, these items are set aside at the request of professors and instructors. Students are allowed to use them only in the library, and only library staff may retrieve them.
- **Closed stacks**—Only library staff are allowed to retrieve items from closed stacks (shelves). In these cases, you must note the relevant location information and ask that the item be retrieved for you.

Subject heading: Usually listed in the "details" portion of a library record (and also on the back of a book's title page, under the heading "Cataloging in Publication"), these headings can be used to help you search for more resources. Books with similar content usually share the same subject headings. You could add these headings to your list of key words (page 25) or start a new list. Later on you can search the catalog for these headings to find more sources.

Availability: This tells you whether the item is available for borrowing. Common availability statuses are as follows:

- **In library**—You can go to the shelf or stack aisle and retrieve the item yourself.
- **On loan**—The due date lets you know when you can expect the item to be back so you can borrow it.
- **REF or R**—This is a common code used to distinguish items housed in the reference section of the library. These items cannot be signed out because they are heavily used and therefore need to remain in the library building.
- **Date:** When was the item published? This information is important to know if you need a particular edition of a book or want only recent sources.
- **Publisher:** This information becomes important when evaluating sources (see page 65). As you get further into your research, you may find that certain publishers seem to specialize in a particular field; think about tracking this information as well.
- **Format:** Is the item a book, an e-book, an audiobook, a CD, a DVD, a microfiche, an online database, a journal, or another format?
- **Description:** This will tell you the number of pages in a book, a CD's running time, and so on. If you're looking for an abridged version of a text, this is where you'll probably find that information.

Don't Forget to Browse!

Believe it or not, browsing the shelves in your favorite library for a promising title can sometimes be less time-consuming than searching online. Sure, you'll have to actually visit the library building, but you won't be sorry you did because browsing can be both fun and productive. Here are some general browsing tips:

- **Be serendipitous:** If you find yourself enjoying a particular book, let its call number lead you into the stacks to browse for hidden gems. If a random title catches your eye, take the book off the shelf and skim its table of contents and index for key words related to your topic. You'll learn more about skimming in Section 3 (page 67). Browsing the shelves is a great way to serendipitously be led to a resource that you would have otherwise missed in an online search.

- **Beeline it to the bound volumes:** Head into the stacks to locate the print copies of journals or magazines appropriate for your research. If these hardcover volumes are kept in the library's closed stacks, just ask one of the library staff to retrieve them for you. Not only do these print editions allow you to experience the color and layout of the original publications (not available in all online sources), but you can also skim the volume's table of contents, browsing for relevant articles.

Chase Those Footnotes!

When you find a good source, make sure you take full advantage of it. Look at the works cited in it to determine what sources that writer relied on, and learn from those choices. Tracking down the sources you find in footnotes and bibliographies can be a very productive pursuit, leading you to additional relevant and authoritative resources.

To Database or Not to Database?

A database is an organized collection of data stored in a computer. Online databases are often paid subscription services that are available through libraries and offer a searchable selection of newspapers, magazines, and journals. Before we get into why you might want to search a database, let's look at different types of databases and examples:

- **Bibliographic databases:** These provide information about books, the contents of a particular library, or a collection of book titles.
    - ▶ The library's OPAC is a type of bibliographic database.
    - ▶ WorldCat is the mother of all OPACs, with over 105 million records contributed by all kinds of libraries around the world. If you can't find a record in WorldCat, it's going to be pretty hard to find that record anywhere.
- **Subject-specific databases:** Each of these databases is a compilation of published material that was gathered on a particular topic or is relevant to one discipline. To identify these types of databases, you can visit the library website of any major

university and look for a section called "subject guides" or "resources by subject." If you can't find anything like that, just ask your local librarian.

> ► For example, PsycINFO is a popular database of information on the literature of psychology and behavioral sciences.

- **Numeric databases:** Here's where you go when you want to find statistics or other data. Governments usually collect and publish this sort of information.

> ► LexisNexis Statistical is a popular numeric database.
>
> ► In Canada, Statistics Canada provides statistical data in many formats.

Why Databases?

When you can already find so much without going too far beyond Google, Yahoo!, and a few other easy-to-access sources, you might wonder why you should bother with databases. Here are some reasons:

- **Academic research:** Academic research is not yet the easiest thing to find on the Web, but because it is authoritative and credible, academic material that is formally published is desirable. Databases really are the best choice when searching for academic research.
- **Complex searches:** Databases can be the best route when you are using many search terms or have many search criteria.
- **Cross-disciplinary searches:** Some databases allow you to choose the disciplines in which to search. So, for example, if you were writing a paper on slavery in West Africa, you might consider searching journals associated with the disciplines of anthropology, geography, African studies, history, and sociology.
- **Repeated searches:** Unlike Web search engines, many subscription databases allow you to save complex search

options. Read on to get more information on how to do this. Databases are big business. As a result, their publishers often ensure that only authorized users have access to the databases. So, if you're logging in to a library database from home, you may need to enter your student or library card number.

Open Access Journals

So what's the difference between a database, the Internet, and an open access journal? The Directory of Open Access Journals (DOAJ) defines the last as journals for which readers and institutions are not charged for access. Although there are a number of different types of open access journals, at their core they each strive to produce quality articles free from any access barriers—a noble pursuit indeed. Check out DOAJ for thousands of free, full-text, quality-controlled scientific and scholarly journals.

Become Database-Search Savvy

Once you've learned how to use one database, it becomes easier to learn how to use another. Sometimes commercial databases change their visual interfaces without notice, meaning that the look of a particular database might be different from the last time you accessed it. But don't fear—your knowledge of database searching will increase with practice regardless of the specific database you're using or any sudden changes in appearance.

Most subscription databases allow you to rank results by different factors, including relevance, publication date, or number of times the source has been cited in other academic works. Every database works a bit differently and has a different look, but many databases share the following features:

Search-saving option: If you sign up for a free database account, you can start saving your complex searches. This is handy especially when you are working on a research project spanning a couple of weeks or longer, or if you are simply perfecting your searching technique. The more you refine your search, the more often you should save it. You can also run a recent search again if you indicated you wanted that search to be saved. Note: if you leave a database without saving your searches, you lose this valuable information about previous searches.

Alerting services: You can choose to be alerted when new articles containing your precise search terms are added to the database. You can ask to be alerted daily, weekly, or monthly via e-mail or really simple syndication (RSS) feed.

Retrieving options: There are a number of ways to retrieve the information in databases. You can usually view a full-text article, print it, or e-mail it to yourself. As well, you can e-mail or save a citation to an article, or export it to a reference management program such as RefWorks or EndNote (see page 18).

Search options: In database searches, you can use some of the same search types that you learned earlier for search engines—for example, Boolean search and word math. However, databases are capable of using higher search functions than search engines. Here are some of these functions:

- **Controlled vocabulary search**—This is definitely a value-added component of commercial databases. Most databases provide a thesaurus or list of subject headings to help users define appropriate subject headings and related subjects.
    - For example, if you were to look up *clothing industry* in a database thesaurus, you would be introduced to related

terms such as *clothing stores, clothing wholesalers, clothing factories, dressmaking, fashion design, secondhand industry,* etc.

- **Proximity searching**—Just like using Boolean operators and word math, proximity searching allows you to specify that your search results include certain terms. Using what's called a *near operator*, you can search for words that appear near or next to one another. Generally, the closer words are in an article, the greater their relevance to one another.
  - ► For example, if you're searching for articles on homeless females and using proximity operators, a database will return records in which the word *homeless* appears within four words of the word *female*.
- **Wildcard symbols**—Different spellings, variant forms, or plural forms of words can be accounted for by using the wildcard operator.
  - ► For example, if you're doing a search for articles on women for your women's studies class, enter the search term *wom*n*. This instructs the database to retrieve results containing the terms *woman, women,* and *womyn*.
- **Field searching**—Unlike search engines, which have only one field in which you can search, databases can let you narrow the search area. Most databases allow you to add or remove fields as you go. Some common searchable fields are
  - ► the full text of articles
  - ► article abstracts only
  - ► articles by a particular author
  - ► images within articles, through a caption search
- **Search limitors**—You can narrow your database searching by a number of factors, including
  - ► item type (e.g., an article or a review)
  - ► language
  - ► publication date
  - ► journal title
  - ► one or more particular disciplines

- ▶ peer-reviewed publications
- ▶ documents with full text
- ▶ documents with images

Knowing the Experts: What the Prof Wrote

Professors publish a lot—it's part of their job to do so. Whether it's been pointed out to you or not, your professor is probably considered an expert in his or her field. So, there's a chance your professor has published about the very topic you are researching. Check it out! Enter his or her name into an online database (using the *author* search field) to see what articles he or she has written. If you find articles relevant to your research, consider using them in your assignment.

The Archive: A Plethora of Primary Sources

Suppose you are doing research on George Washington Carver and want to dig deeper. You could head to the Iowa State University Archives to access his personal papers, including his notes about original research and product development. Or imagine you are doing research into Marshall McLuhan. You could put in a request to Library and Archives Canada to view textual records, photographs, artwork, audiovisual material, and objects related to Marshall McLuhan's career as a communications scholar. Alternatively, you could look through online archives chosen for your research focus, for example, the Online Archive of California.

Note:

- An archive is the place to be if you need to access *primary documents*. (Some archives may also have secondary sources, but these are not the institution's focus.)
- Searching archives is best done after searching online and at libraries because you should already know a fair bit about your topic. You will need to know key facts and dates about your topic to narrow your search in the archive and make the best use of your time.

As laid out in York University's *Archival Research Tutorial*, the major differences between libraries and archives are as follows:

	Archives	Libraries
Materials	unpublished material in the form of unique *records*, which are often one of a kind	published material— books, magazines, journals, and more. This means that multiple copies may be available in other libraries or in bookstores.
Organization	grouped in *fonds*. A fonds is one grouping of unique *records*. Archival materials are arranged in the original order in which their authors intended. As a result, the organization varies widely from one material to the next.	organized by a standard classification system, usually the Dewey Decimal or Library of Congress system. All materials are organized in the same way.
Retrieval Methods	*finding aids*—listings of all the records in a fonds. Finding aids help you know what a collection contains and how to ask for it.	library catalog—helps you know what a collection contains and how to find it on the shelves or ask for it
Borrowing	not available for circulation. You can't take physical records home with you.	often available for circulation. You can borrow many kinds of materials to take home with you.

Record versus Archival Record

Don't let the term *record* confuse you. *Archival records* are completely different from the *catalog records* found in library OPACs. Instead of a listing or representation of the thing being sought (a catalog record in a library), an archival record is the actual item sought by researchers. Here are some examples:

- the personal records of an individual, such as
  - ► letters or e-mails
  - ► photographs
  - ► journals or diaries
  - ► notes and manuscripts
- the corporate records of an organization, such as
  - ► ledgers or account books
  - ► annual reports and project files
  - ► meeting minutes
  - ► legal documents, such as bylaws or letters of incorporation
- evidence of particular actions taken or decisions made by an individual or a group

Fond of Fonds? More about Fonds

A *fonds* is the entire body of records of a person, a family, or an organization. A fonds (a French word) is essentially what you're looking to retrieve when you visit an archive. It's an archivist's job to preserve the context in which the records were created, maintained, and used. This is why each fonds is organized differently.

Who Has What? Locating Fonds

But how would you know which institutions had McLuhan's and Carver's fonds? Or how would you know about the online archive of early advertisements at Duke University?

What excellent questions—I'm glad you asked! You would consult an online research tool that accesses descriptions of archival fonds. Can't find one? Ask your librarian for help. Note, however: there is no single way of getting to archival information online. You need to search for the archive first. (This is partly due to the fact that the term *archive* is interpreted in various ways online.)

Here are two ways to search online:

- by visiting a website that tells you what archives are held where. For example:
  - ► the SCAN online catalog, an electronic database, describing historical records in more than 50 Scottish archives
  - ► Archives Canada, which includes the Canadian Archival Information Network, providing online access to the holdings of over 800 archival institutions across Canada
- by visiting an archive's website. Many archives post their finding aids online, but some prefer to keep paper copies of the finding aids accessible only at their institutions.

How to Read a Finding Aid

To locate items in an archive, you must first consult a *finding aid*. Similar to the details in a library's catalog record, certain parts of a finding aid can help you figure out whether a fonds is relevant to your research. For example, here are the common features of finding aids used in Canadian archival institutions:

- **Title:** the name of the individual or group responsible for creating the records
- **Dates:** the years covered by the material in the fonds
- **Extent:** the amount and format of the records
- **Biographical sketch** or **administrative history:** a brief overview of either the life of the individual or the history of the organization that created the records
- **Scope and content note:** a description of the types of documents in the fonds and their functions, as well as the activities in which the records were used

Using People as Resources

Interviewing someone related to your research focus is a great way to gather information from a primary source. Think about contacting professors, government officials, filmmakers, or members of civic and business organizations. These experts can help by answering questions and referring you to even more sources. Online searches and searches in directories (see page 39) might be just the way to decide whom to approach as resources for your specific research assignment.

Knowing how to conduct a professional interview is a great skill to have. It will serve you well not just in academia but also in your personal or career pursuits. You can conduct an interview in person, over the phone, via e-mail, or with a video call (e.g., Skype). You can use the template Interview Checklist (Grab & Go page 64) to help.

Tips for Personal Interviews

1. **Check it out:** Many colleges and universities have a Human
    Subjects Committee or Ethics Review Committee, which reviews
    all research involving human subjects. If you're thinking of
    using an interview as part of your research, ask your professor,
    instructor, or librarian about your school's research policies
    and procedures related to personal interviews.

2. **Make contact:** After you have identified potential interview
    subjects, introduce yourself and the reason for the proposed
    interview. Help your potential interviewee understand your
    interest in what he or she knows, and demonstrate that you've
    done some preliminary research. This is a great opportunity to
    practice your *elevator pitch*—a short summary of your research
    focus. Be specific about how long you think the interview
    will take, and ask for the subject's permission if you plan to
    audio-record the interview. Make it clear that you will cite the
    interviewee as a source.

3. **Prepare for the interview:** Determining beforehand what
    you specifically want to learn from the interview will make
    extracting that information from your interviewee much more
    efficient. So, it's a good idea to prepare a variety of questions.
    These should be *open-ended* (designed to avoid simple "yes" or
    "no" answers) and crafted to help you stay focused, get the most
    from your interviewee, and avoid getting sidetracked.

4. **During the interview:** If you're unsure of a response given,
    ask for clarification. Be prepared to reformulate the question if
    necessary. Remember, you can always reread an article if you
    don't understand a passage, but you can't redo an interview!

5. **After the interview:** Send a thank-you card or e-mail. It's
    important to thank the interviewee for his or her time. The
    research community is a small one, and anything you can do
    to foster positive relations in it is a good idea.

6. **Cite your interview:** Don't forget to cite your interview as a
    source, and quote with care.

Whither Shall I Wander?
Reflecting on Locating Sources

Think back on where you have searched and what sources you have found.

The Internet is a great place to start your research, but if you don't go past using the Internet, you'll never achieve research virtuoso status. Finding tertiary sources on the Web is a good first step and can help you identify the secondary and primary sources required in the later stages of the research process.

The library is the next stop on the road to attaining virtuoso standing. Here's where you can find some great secondary sources and maybe even some primary resources. Don't forget to ask for help from your local librarian, take time to browse, and take advantage of the research tools offered by your library's website.

Get out there and visit an archive. This is an activity best suited to the later stages of your research. This extra step, however, is sure to garner you respect among your fellow researchers, cementing your place in the research virtuoso community.

Finally, consider the people around you. Are any of them experts in the research field you are exploring? Perhaps you might interview them and create some primary research on your own.

How did the search go? If you think that there are more places to search and sources to find—or if you want to return to earlier stages in the research process—now is a perfect time.

Get Organized Checklist:
Digging In

GRAB & GO

- ☐ I have thought about the source requirements of the assignment and how much is enough.

- ☐ I understand the differences among primary, secondary, and tertiary sources.

- ☐ I know how to effectively use search operators in a Web search engine.

- ☐ I have investigated a number of subject directories that could help with my research.

- ☐ I have acquainted myself with the library's website and its various research support tools.

- ☐ I understand how to use a library catalog effectively.

- ☐ I have begun to compile a list of relevant library call numbers and subject headings.

- ☐ I have taken the time to browse the library's shelves (stacks).

- ☐ I understand how to effectively search a database.

- ☐ I understand what archives have to offer and how to use an archival finding aid.

- ☐ I have considered how to conduct personal interviews for my research.

- ☐ I have reflected on the research process and on where and how to locate sources.

Creating an Effective Search String

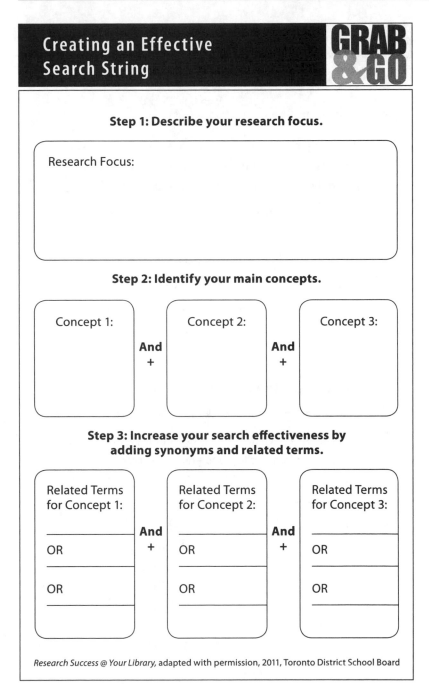

Step 1: Describe your research focus.

Research Focus:

Step 2: Identify your main concepts.

Concept 1:

And +

Concept 2:

And +

Concept 3:

Step 3: Increase your search effectiveness by adding synonyms and related terms.

Related Terms for Concept 1:

_____

OR

_____

OR

_____

And +

Related Terms for Concept 2:

_____

OR

_____

OR

_____

And +

Related Terms for Concept 3:

_____

OR

_____

OR

_____

Research Success @ Your Library, adapted with permission, 2011, Toronto District School Board

Interview Checklist

GRAB & GO

Before the Interview

- ☐ When requesting an interview via telephone or e-mail, demonstrate some prior knowledge of your interviewee and/or his or her institution/organization.
- ☐ Inform your interviewee of the approximate length of the interview.
- ☐ Prepare a list of open-ended questions.
- ☐ Practice your research "elevator pitch."
- ☐ Ask for permission to audio-record the interview.

During the Interview

- ☐ Thank the interviewee for his or her time.
- ☐ Reformulate questions or ask for clarification if necessary.
- ☐ If recording, check the beginning, middle, and end of the audio file before you leave to ensure the recording was successful.

After the Interview

- ☐ Send a thank-you card or e-mail.

Taking Stock: Evaluating and Processing Information

Okay, it's time to take stock of what you've gathered so far in your research assignment. On the journey to becoming a research virtuoso, evaluating what you have and starting to put it together (in a research paper or another format) is just as necessary as developing a research focus and gathering sources!

To start evaluating the sources you've located, you'll first need to look them over and determine which are the most useful. Skimming and scanning for relevant information will not only save you time but will also help you determine how certain information and ideas can fit into the format for communicating your research.

65

Skimming and Scanning

Skimming and scanning are speed-reading techniques.

Skimming

Skimming gives you a *general sense* of the text and an *overview of its contents*. Skimming is quickly reading *across* a text to understand its main ideas. Here are some common approaches to skimming:

FOR **BOOKS**
- reading the title page to locate information such as the date of publication, the publisher, the author's credentials, etc.
- skimming the back cover or dust jacket for summary information or for biographical information about the author
- skimming the preface or introduction
- reading the opening or closing paragraphs of selected chapters, where the main ideas are usually introduced and repeated
- consulting the index and the table of contents for specific references to the research topic

FOR **ARTICLES** OR **CHAPTERS**
- reading the title and the headings
- reading any *italic*, **bold**, or underlined words first
- skimming through the entire document to get a general impression of its length and organization
- consulting all illustrations, charts, graphs, and so on
- reading the first and last paragraphs

FOR **WEBSITES**
- browsing the site's home page
- identifying who created a site by visiting the home page or About Us page
- browsing the various pages of the site to see if they meet your needs

Scanning

Scanning helps you *locate a specific piece of information* before reading the entire source. Scanning involves quickly reading *down* a page to find a specific word, detail, or fact. Before scanning a text, refer to your bank of key words (Grab & Go page 25) to remind yourself what exactly you are searching for.

Some common things to look for as you scan are

- headings
- names of people or organizations
- facts
- statistics
- dates
- key words and their synonyms

The ABCs of Evaluation

Your research assignment will be judged largely on the basis of the quality of your information. As you find potential sources, it's important to consider whether each one is reliable and appropriate for your topic. This book uses the ABC structure to discuss evaluating sources—judging a source by its author and authority, its body, and its currency.

A – Author and Authority: Can you trust the author? What makes him or her an authority?

B – Body: When evaluating the body of a source, consider the following:

- objectivity
- accuracy
- completeness

- relevancy
- format

C – **Currency:** How current is the information?

On the following pages, you will see tips for evaluating websites, databases, and print sources with the ABCs and key questions.

Evaluating Online Sources with the ABCs

Evaluating all of your sources is important, but perhaps this is most difficult (and most critical) for online resources because the Internet is like the Wild West of the information universe. Anyone accessing an Internet connection can post something online—whether that person is an expert sitting in an ivory tower or an oddball sitting in a basement—so there is a lot of inaccurate, out-of-date, biased, and even offensive information on the Web.

However, even if a source is not the best one for your research, it may still prove useful to you. For example, it might give background information, lead you to a more promising source, or provide key words you haven't already thought of.

Here are some questions to ask about websites using the ABCs:

Author and Authority

- Is an author identified? If so, who is the author? The author could be a person, group of people, or organization. This information is usually found on the home page or in the About Us page. (If you can't find a link to the site's home page, retype the URL (Web address) up to the first forward slash (/) to bring you there.)
- What credentials are noted for the author(s)?
- What contact information (e-mail, phone, or postal address) is provided for the author(s)? Are comments or other types of feedback solicited? When a source provides contact information and solicits feedback, that indicates a willingness to be held accountable for the contents.

(Continued)

Author and Authority

- Can you check the author and contact information through other sources to confirm they exist—e.g., through a directory?
- Does the URL give any indication of who runs the site and its authority? (For example, a URL ending with .gov for a U.S. government site; see page 38 for a listing.)
- Have links been made to the website or web page from credible sources? To check this, perform a link search using a web search engine. To do this, type in *link:* followed by the Web address of the site in question. For example, enter *link:http://library.duke.edu/digitalcollections/* into a search engine and it will retrieve a number of different websites that link to Duke University's Digital Collections website.

Body

Objectivity	• Does the author clearly distinguish fact from theory, conclusions, or opinions? • Part of evaluating a website is evaluating its focus, perspective, and bias. ▷ For example, if you were doing research on the 2010 oil spill in the Gulf of Mexico, you would expect to see substantiated facts and balanced perspectives in an online news report, an opinion in a news columnist's editorial, a certain perspective on the website for the oil giant BP (British Petroleum), and a different perspective on the website of Greenpeace. An individual writing a personal blog about cleaning beaches during the spill would present another perspective and a narrow focus. • Consider what the purpose of the website might be. ▷ For instance, a commercial site with a lot of ads and banners is trying to sell you products. Go to the home page to get a better idea of the goals of the overall site.
Accuracy	• On initial review, does the site appear well researched? What leads you to that conclusion? • Does the site or page provide documented support for information presented as fact? (Check the bottom of the web page to see if there are footnotes to other publications; this is usually an indication of a well-researched website. Just because the information appears on the Internet doesn't mean it shouldn't include citations to other works.)

	• Is the information on the site accurate? You can verify the accuracy of the information by consulting other print or electronic resources. • Are there misspellings? Misspellings are a possible indicator of poor-quality publications for both online and print sources.
Relevancy	• Does the website have a site map on which you can check where relevant information might be found? (A link to a site map page can usually be found at the very bottom of a website's home page.) • Does the site have a built-in search engine? If so, search for key words within the site for relevant pages. If not, scan the site for relevant words and information.
Currency	
Dates	• When was the information created, and when was it last updated? The date of the last update can usually be found at the bottom of a web page. Avoid using information from a web page that doesn't mention this information.
Links	• Are the links working or dead (broken)? On a website, always test the links to other websites. Links that no longer work can indicate that the source is not maintained, and this suggests that it may be unreliable.

Evaluating Wikipedia

Wikipedia is a popular, free-to-use, online encyclopedia that is freely created and maintained. Using a particular software tool called a *wiki* (the Hawaiian word for *quick*), this unique collaborative project was launched in 2001. Wikipedia encourages anyone with an Internet connection to contribute posts freely and to edit entries posted by other writers; Wikipedia is controversial in part because of this fact. Because individuals don't need any credentials to participate in writing the encyclopedia, most professors believe Wikipedia entries should not be accepted as authoritative.

Although there have been many successes for Wikipedia, it has also been plagued by vandalism. For example, pranksters altering Wikipedia entries have been particularly unkind to former British prime minister Tony Blair. The entry for Blair was changed to give his middle name as "Whoop-de-Doo," and it asserted that he had a collection of Hitler posters as a teenager—among other misinformation.

Despite these risks, Wikipedia does have its uses:

- Its entries are a great place to pick up key words about your topic.
- Its entries can lead you to authoritative information someplace else.
- The citations in Wikipedia entries can help familiarize you with the types of sources out there.
- Wikipedia's discussion tabs can alert you to contentious issues surrounding your subject. (For a good example of this, check out the discussion page for Wikipedia's entry on Adolf Hitler.) These tabs allow the content of an encyclopedia article to be separated from communal discussions of the subject.

Use the FIND Function

Does learning a new keyboard shortcut make your day? If so, you'll love this one: hold down the *CTRL* or *Control* key while you press the *F* key to find a word or a phrase in an electronic document. This is a perfect function to use when browsing a website for key words.

Evaluating Databases with the ABCs

When it comes to doing research, databases trump Web search engines most of the time due to authority and credibility. One advantage of databases is that the articles, reports, and other documents in them have already been published elsewhere, so their original publishers have already evaluated the contents for quality. This is especially true of journal articles, which are often refereed, or peer-reviewed; in other words, experts in a particular field have vetted the articles. In addition, database vendors have filtered the items for reliability when opting to include them in their products.

So why should you care about evaluating the information in these sources? Well, because not all databases are created equal! The following ABCs are for evaluating databases and they direct you further to evaluate each source you find on a database.

Author and Authority

- Does the database appear in a librarian-authored research guide? If so, this is a good sign! (Remember: these guides can be found on academic library websites.)
- Once you evaluate a database with the ABCs and decide it deserves another look, you can evaluate a possible source found on that database using the ABCs for evaluating print sources (see page 75).

Body

Completeness	• How searchable is the database? • Does it offer a controlled vocabulary to focus your search? • Which fields are searchable? • Can you search by article type—e.g., book review, scholarly publication? • Does the database have an online help function or an online tutorial?

Relevancy	• What topical areas does the database cover?
	• Does it have a subject emphasis or is it multidisciplinary? (If you can't find this information on your own, just ask a librarian.)
	• For what audience were the documents in the database chosen? Is the intended audience for the database students up to grade 12, under-graduates, graduate students, or the lay public? Once again, consult a librarian if you're unsure.
	• Consider the type of material included in the database. Some databases might include the following:
	  ▷ popular sources—newspapers and general magazines
	  ▷ trade journals
	  ▷ scholarly publications
	  ▷ articles with images
	  ▷ theses and dissertations
	  ▷ conference proceedings
	  ▷ government documents

Format	• In what formats do the documents in the database appear?
	  ▷ full text
	  ▷ PDF
	  ▷ HTML

- How much information is provided by the database?
  - ▷ citations only
  - ▷ citations and article abstracts
  - ▷ citations and full-text articles

Currency

- Does the database have current or retrospective coverage of materials?
- How far back does its indexing of documents go?

Evaluating Print Sources with the ABCs

Reference books in print form and found in libraries are generally reliable in themselves, and you can use them to evaluate other library materials. For example, you could use a reference book in a library to spot-check the accuracy of an author's facts and figures in another print source. Here are more ways to evaluate print sources:

Author and Authority

- What makes the author an expert in his or her field?
- What in his or her biographical information, credentials, or affiliations indicates authority?
- Is this a peer-reviewed source? Peer-reviewed journals review the credentials and expertise of contributing authors before accepting articles for publication, so if the article is found in one of these periodicals, you can take that as a sign of its reliability.
- Does the material appear in a source edited by a well-known authority? (Authors who don't yet have strong credentials can build a reputation by having their work published in anthologies or journals that are edited by well-known authorities.)
- Who is the publisher of the work, and what is the publisher's reputation in this field? Consider the difference between academic presses (i.e., at a university) and commercial publishers. Most university presses can be considered reliable, especially if you recognize the name of the university.

(Continued)

75

- Has the source been reviewed? If so, where? Does the review note the work as authoritative? The following can direct you to reputable reviews in print: *Book Review Digest, Book Review Index,* and *Ulrich's Periodical Directory.* For online reviews see *Booklist, Library Journal,* and *Publishers Weekly.*

Body	
Objectivity	• Does the author clearly distinguish fact from theory, conclusions, or opinions? • What form is the source, and what are the expectations of that form? For example, a news report is expected to include verifiable facts and possibly some quoted opinions, but an editorial is expected to present an opinion with or without support. • Is the author's purpose clearly stated? Is the author's intent to survey current findings and thinking on a topic, to promote his or her beliefs, or to comment from a personal perspective on the subject? Consider the difference between information and propaganda, for example: information simply communicates knowledge, while propaganda tries to instill a particular attitude or response and is promoted by an interested party.
Accuracy	• On initial review, does the site appear well researched? What leads you to that conclusion? • Is the information accurate? To verify the information, use other sources. Some common elements to verify include statistical data, dates, and any statements that contradict what you have learned from other sources. • Are there misspellings? Misspellings are a possible indicator of poor-quality publications for both online and print sources.
Completeness	• Does the source include documentation—a reference list or works cited list? • If not, are the author's sources acknowledged in some other credible way? • Has the author used sources that are respected and authoritative?

Relevancy	• Does the source contain the type of information you need?
	• Is it aimed at readers like you? For example:
	  ▷ Is the language very academic or technical? Too basic?
	  ▷ Do visuals such as maps and scientific diagrams provide the right amount of detail for your needs?

Format	• Does the work include the type of material you need? For example, you might be looking for the following:
	  ▷ statistics
	  ▷ original research
	  ▷ summarized information from other, documented sources
	  ▷ primary sources or quotations from primary sources
	  ▷ opinion pieces or editorials
	  ▷ visuals such as maps, diagrams, or photographs

Currency

- When was the source published? (If you need the most recent publications on a subject, database collections may have more articles to choose from than the print periodical collections in your library.)
- Consider when the source was last revised. Textbooks, research guides, and reference works are often revised and updated several times. Be sure you're using the most recent edition if you need current information.

Note-Taking: Get Those Thoughts in Order!

Now that you've evaluated the sources and information you've found, it's time to read and take notes. Note-taking is when you'll start to organize the information you've discovered so far, laying the groundwork for a strong research paper (or whatever format your communication will take).

Note-taking is crucial to the research process. The activity itself demonstrates your understanding of the material. By choosing what to summarize, quote, and paraphrase, and by putting information into your own words, you're implementing the higher-order thinking skills in Bloom's Taxonomy. So make Bloom proud and take good notes!

Taking notes is not just about evaluating someone else's work—it's at this stage of the game when you'll also be evaluating your own ideas. To do this, you must revisit the research focus you started with and tweak it in light of the information you've come across. For example, ask yourself:

- Are your earlier assumptions still valid?
- Do you need to revise your research focus?
- Is an original perspective on your research focus emerging?

Plagiarism and How Sloppy Notes Led to One Sorry Writer

In a research article for *Journalism and Mass Communications Quarterly,* Norman P. Lewis presented findings that problematic techniques, including sloppy note-taking, often lead to acts of plagiarism. Lewis cited the example of a *New York Times* writer whose sloppy note-taking caused him to mistake two paragraphs from a magazine as his own interview observations. After publishing this faulty story, the *Times* had to issue a public apology clarifying the situation and acknowledging the mistakenly uncredited material from the magazine. Imagine the embarrassment and implications for that journalist!

Different schools define plagiarism and its consequences differently. Look at your school's definition of plagiarism. Regulations, guidelines, and procedures regarding plagiarism can be found on your school's website. Further information is also included in course handbooks and handouts from professors, librarians, and academic departments. And we look at plagiarism again on page 85.

Notes on Note-Taking

There are three main purposes to taking notes: summarizing, quoting, and paraphrasing. These purposes correspond with different types of notes.

Summary Notes

The purpose of summary notes is to understand the main points of an article or a book.

- These are the types of notes in which you lay out ideas, details, and arguments in point form.

- If you have printed out an article, making notes in the margins might also help you to summarize the main points.

Shorthand's the Way 2 Go

Because summary notes are supposed to be brief, knowing and using certain symbols and abbreviations can save time and space. Consider using the following:

Symbol or Abbreviation	To Mean ...
+ *or* &	and *or* plus
=	equals
>	greater than, more, *or* larger
<	less than, fewer than, *or* smaller
w/	with
w/in	within
w/o	without
b/c	because
2	to
→	leads to, produces, *or* results in
←	comes from

Direct Quotes

Jot down exact quotes in some distinctive way (e.g., between quotation marks, enclosed in parentheses). The index-card technique described below is a fantastic way to keep track of direct quotes that you intend to use in your research paper. Take care to identify quotations as such (see pages 81–82).

Paraphrasing Notes

These types of notes help you put someone else's ideas into your own words. Hop on over to page 90 for more about paraphrasing. Paraphrasing (and properly crediting sources) can help steer you away from using too many direct quotations in a research paper. After all, it is *your* paper—so use *your* own words!

How to Take Notes

Following are some ideas on how to keep your notes organized throughout the research process—and by extension, how to keep you organized.

Index cards: Index cards are a great way to keep your notes short and sweet. Because the size of these cards limits how much information they can contain, they force you to be concise. Here is a sample with suggestions on what to include:

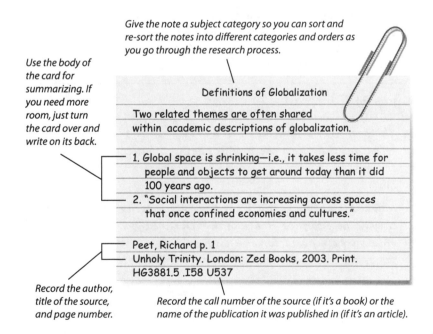

Give the note a subject category so you can sort and re-sort the notes into different categories and orders as you go through the research process.

Use the body of the card for summarizing. If you need more room, just turn the card over and write on its back.

Definitions of Globalization

Two related themes are often shared within academic descriptions of globalization.

1. Global space is shrinking—i.e., it takes less time for people and objects to get around today than it did 100 years ago.
2. "Social interactions are increasing across spaces that once confined economies and cultures."

Peet, Richard p. 1
Unholy Trinity. London: Zed Books, 2003. Print.
HG3881.5 .I58 U537

Record the author, title of the source, and page number.

Record the call number of the source (if it's a book) or the name of the publication it was published in (if it's an article).

Note template: You can use the template Taking Notes (Grab &
Go page 96) to write notes. Here's a sample with notes on one source:

Taking Notes

Legend:	Q – Quote	P – Paraphrase	ME – My insights

Citation: McLuhan, Marshall, and W. Terrence Gordon.
Understanding Media: The Extensions of Man. Corte
Madera, CA: Gingko Press, 2003.

Call number:	☒ Academic Library	☐ Online
P90 .M26 2003	☐ Public Library	☐ Other

Q *p. 59*

*"As the age of information demands the simultaneous use
of all our faculties, we discover that we are most at leisure
when we are most intensely involved, very much as with
the artists in all ages."*

P *p. 19*

*The process of production has a greater influence on human
relations than does the product being produced.*

ME

*Nowadays people spend more time socializing online than
they do face-to-face. How has this changed our perceptions
of leisure time and community?*

Sticky notes: Jot down one main idea (key event, organization, etc.) per sticky note and sort each one underneath a main column. Below is an illustration of where a session with sticky notes can lead you. You can stick these notes to a wall or on a table and arrange and rearrange them as necessary.

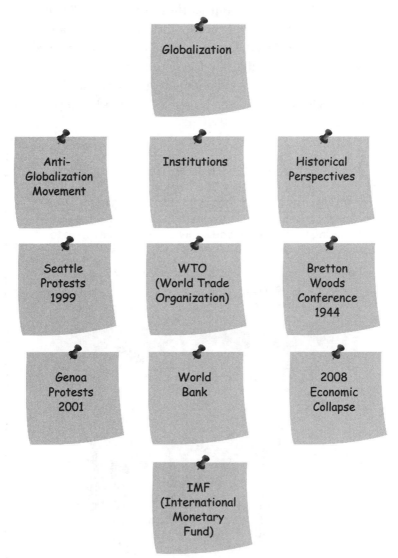

Note-taking software and applications: The following electronic tools can help you gather facts and manage your sources. Both tools have free and paid account options.

- **Mindola SuperNotecard:** If you like the idea of using index cards but want to transfer the technique to a digital environment, try SuperNotecard. These virtual note cards can be organized on the screen, placed in decks, or grouped and categorized just like physical note cards.
- **Evernote:** This cloud-based note-taking application allows you to add multiple searchable and sortable tags to each note you create.

Saving Your Work—in the Clouds?

For any given assignment, once you start making notes, organizing them, and drafting on a computer, you must also start saving the results. As you know, there are many ways to save your work digitally. Here are some examples:

- move files onto a USB (universal serial bus) key
- e-mail files to yourself
- save files in *the cloud*

Cloud computing is computing on the Internet and a way of using the Internet for your computing needs. In this case, *saving work to the cloud* means saving digital files online and away from your physical location.

Online storage is a great way to ensure that your work is backed up and accessible from anywhere. So, if your computer breaks down—and if you've saved your work using a cloud computing application such as Dropbox, Box.net, or Google Docs—then don't worry about your saved work; it will still be accessible through the cloud.

Staying Honest: Crediting Your Sources and Avoiding Plagiarism

Properly giving credit where it is due is a key principle in research, and universities and colleges have very strong policies about crediting sources and against plagiarism.

Although the specifics of how to cite sources varies (see page 92), the purposes of citing sources remain the same. The main reasons include the following:

1. **Staying honest:** By citing your sources, you give credit where it belongs and ward off accusations of plagiarism. Avoid taking the credit for someone else's words, original ideas, and original expressions by being honest about what you've borrowed.
2. **Building trust:** As you've already learned from the ABCs approach to evaluating sources, your readers will look to your citations to decide how much they can trust your work.
3. **Creating a path:** Responsible researchers provide their readers with a way of accessing the earlier research that has informed

the work being read. By citing these sources, you're showing your reader how your work connects with that of other researchers, leading to the final purpose of citation . . .

4. **Building community:** Part of being a research virtuoso is establishing yourself in a community of researchers. When you cite sources fully and accurately, you are helping to build both the scholarly and the social value of the research community.

Properly giving credit may seem simple at first, but it gets tricky from time to time.

Generally, the following do not require citations:	However, what must be credited includes the following:
• dates • simple definitions • commonly known observations and facts	• quoted ideas and information • paraphrased ideas and information • statistics • sources that are not text-based, such as photographs, artwork, radio programs, maps, videos, and even interviews that you conduct

The information you need to record to credit your sources is called bibliographic data. The template Bibliographic Data Tracker (Grab & Go pages 97–98) can help you record this information.

- **For printed books** the data you need includes author(s), full title (including any subtitle), editor(s), publisher, location of the publisher (always choose the first one that appears), and date of publication.
- **For articles** this data includes the page numbers of the article, author(s), article title, title of the journal/magazine/newspaper,

volume and issue number for that publication, and publication date.

- **For online sources** this data includes website address (URL), date you accessed it, and name of the database (if applicable).

If you find it too tedious to record these details, consider photo-copying a book's title page and its reverse side, which is where copy-right information is listed. Similarly, for a journal article, you could photocopy the masthead of the publication. Be sure to write down the page numbers of any quotations you are using. (You could add page numbers to the photocopy or write them in your notes.) While you're at it, why not jot down the location information (call number, shelving area, etc.) somewhere on this photocopy so you can track down the source later on.

Turnitin.com: What's Your View?

Turnitin.com is an anti-plagiarism service used by many North American universities. Professors use it to compare students' assignments with billions of pages of assignment papers and other documents in a database. This service then reports back on sections in a student's assignment that may have been plagiarized.

Some students disagree with the widespread use of this service. Their criticisms stem from a belief that the tool promotes and institutionalizes a presumption that some students will plagiarize. Some critics also consider the use of the service an invasion of privacy. Turnitin.com and the controversy around it certainly provide food for thought.

Creative Commons

According to the organization's website, Creative Commons is a way to balance the reality of the Internet with the reality of copyright laws. This nonprofit organization is helping to grow a "digital commons"—a pool of content that can be copied, distributed, and built upon legally—within the boundaries of copyright law. Creative Commons (and the Creative Commons licenses, which you will read about next) relates to all sorts of copyrighted materials, including visual images. For more information, check out the Creative Commons website.

So, suppose you are looking for an image to use in a presentation. Act responsibly and seek out a Creative Commons image. Flickr (an image-hosting website), for example, allows you to browse or search through content covered by Creative Commons licensing. When you find a picture you really like, right-click on the *some rights reserved* link to determine which type of license applies.

Two popular forms of Creative Commons licenses are the following:

- **Attribution license:** You can copy, distribute, and display the image as long as you credit where it came from.
- **Non-commercial license:** You can do the above but for non-commercial purposes only.

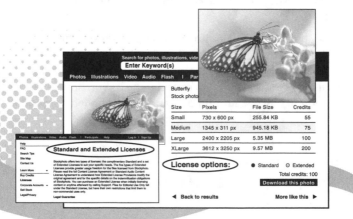

Avoiding Plagiarism

Below are some tips that can help you steer clear of plagiarizing and avoid allegations of plagiarism.

1. **Understand the word:** *Plagiarism* (Latin for *kidnapper*) occurs when someone uses or passes off another person's words, original ideas, or original expressions as though they were his or her own. Plagiarizing can be an intentional or an unintentional act. As noted earlier, check your school's definition of plagiarism and policies about it. Every university and college will have its own explanation of plagiarism; it pays to be aware in advance. Know that the penalties can be severe: anything from failure in that course to expulsion from the institution. If you are interested, scan the policies of noted institutions online to get a sense of the important standing academic honesty has in the scholarly world.

2. **Manage your time:** Anxiety is fertile ground for plagiarism. Many researchers have been tempted to plagiarize when they find themselves running out of time—for example, when they feel unable to come up with their own ideas or feel too rushed to properly and accurately credit the sources used in formulating their ideas. Here are some time-management tips to avoid this problem:

   ▶ *Break up the writing process:* Nobody can write all the time. Every writer needs time away from his or her paper to gain some perspective. But these breaks don't have to be unproductive! Take the opportunity to go over your references and tidy up any loose ends. Or work on an entirely different task to get some fresh ideas percolating on this one.

   ▶ *Start early and set up your source notes early:* See pages 10–11 for tips on scheduling and pages 97–98 for tips on tracking sources and citations.

3. **Stay in control:** You risk plagiarizing when you lose track of which words and ideas are yours and which are not. Here's where good note-taking techniques are crucial.

   ▶ *In your notes and files, carefully distinguish between direct quotations, paraphrasing, summarizing, and your own ideas from the get-go.* You are more likely to stay on top of things right from the beginning.

   ▶ *If you are copying and pasting from electronic sources, keep track of every change to an electronic file.* Clearly identify sources, place direct quotations in quotation marks, and mark your electronic notes with labels such as *source, direct quotation, paraphrase, summary,* and *my idea.*

4. **Know when to paraphrase:** If you think you can explain an idea better (for example, in a way that is clearer or more succinct) than the source in which you encountered that idea, then it's time to paraphrase. To do this, take an author's idea, select what's most significant to your research, and restate it in your own words, but still credit the source.

   ▶ *Cite it right:* Aside from crediting the work you're paraphrasing in your works cited list or bibliography, you must also include in-text citations. To learn more about when and how to use these types of citations, check citation styles (pages 92–93).

   ▶ *Compare the original and paraphrase:* Effective paraphrasing involves more than simply replacing a word here and there or checking a thesaurus for substitutes. (Students risk being charged with plagiarism when they follow a source too closely in their paraphrase.) To avoid poor paraphrasing, consider the following:

      ▷ Double-check your wording against the original passage. Mark with a highlighter what remains the same.

      ▷ Read your paraphrase aloud. Note where the expression sounds natural to how you normally write and where it doesn't.

▷ Consider using quotation marks in your paraphrasing notes to identify particular phrases or words that you've borrowed directly from the source and that must remain for sense or clarity.

5. **Know when to quote:** You should record exact quotations from a source in the following instances:

    ▶ if the original words of the author express the idea that you are trying to communicate clearly and succinctly, and you're worried that paraphrasing will only muddle the message

    ▶ when the author states a view you disagree with; it's only fair to record that view exactly as it was written before you pull it apart.

    ▶ when you can't yet decide whether to quote directly or paraphrase because your research is not far enough along; if you quote directly while noting sources, you can always turn the direct quotation into a paraphrase later, but changing your mind about a paraphrase will be harder!

No Word Twisting: Don't Manipulate Those Quotes!

To be a research virtuoso, you will have to respect the quotations you use. Part of upholding your academic integrity is maintaining the integrity of each chosen quote. This means not taking a quotation out of context, not shortening it unnecessarily, and not rearranging it except for grammatical purposes.

Check your school's policies and procedures for changing quotations.

Dueling Citation Styles

With so many ways to cite sources out there, how do you know which is the right style to use? The short answer is to ask your professor (or instructor, etc.). Although certain citation styles are favored by particular disciplines, some professors will allow you to use whichever style you prefer as long as you use it consistently and correctly throughout the research assignment.

The most popular citation styles for academic research are as follows:

Chicago Style	• Here, *Chicago* refers to University of Chicago Press publications. *The Chicago Manual of Style* presents two citation systems: • notes and bibliography system—often favored when writing about literature, history, and the arts • author-date system—often favored when writing about the sciences (physical, natural, social) Sometimes professors also point to another style described in University of Chicago Press publications—Turabian style. Remember to clarify with your professor, instructor, TA, etc., which specific Chicago style is required, and then refer to the latest style guide in your library.
APA Style	Commonly used in the natural and social sciences, American Psychological Association (APA) style lists the date of publication front and center. Because these academic fields change rapidly, it's important for readers to quickly determine how old a source is. This style is also common to nursing and business studies. Refer to the latest edition of the *Publication Manual of the American Psychological Association* for a guide to using APA style.

MLA Style	Commonly used in the humanities, Modern Language Association (MLA) style doesn't place as much importance on the date of publication as does APA. Generally, the emphasis in this field is not necessarily on new research. The *MLA Handbook for Writers of Research Papers* will bring you up to speed on the formatting requirements of MLA style.

Citation styles are forever changing, evolving over time to adapt to different media (think URLs and YouTube videos) used for research. For the most up-to-date information on your citation style of choice, check your university or college bookstore for the latest editions of the style guides mentioned above, or access them through your school's writing center or online. Purdue University's Online Writing Lab (OWL) is a great source for many subjects, including formatting in APA and MLA styles.

WorldCat: A Friendly Citation Feline

Remember reading about WorldCat way back in Section 2? Well, besides being the mother of all bibliographic databases, this free online resource can help you formulate proper citations. Each WorldCat entry comes with a *cite/export* option. If you choose this option, a pop-up box appears that allows you to copy a formatted citation for the book, DVD, CD, article, etc., in your choice of certain official styles.

Think Insight—Not Access

Once upon a time, information was considered a scarce resource. For most of human history, information in the form of the written word was very expensive to distribute. After the invention of the printing press way back in the 15th century, costs came down. Fast-forward to the widespread use of the Internet in the late 20th century, and well, distribution costs pretty much evaporated. So, in today's information-rich society, access to information is not so much the issue. Instead, *insight into that information* is becoming a scarce resource in the 21st century.

The virtuoso's challenge is to sort through information with agility and integrity. Speed-reading strategies, the ABCs of evaluation, note-taking techniques, and citation styles are all tools in your arsenal to gain an accurate and deep understanding of the information you seek.

Get Organized Checklist: *Taking Stock*

☐ I have skimmed and scanned the sources I've collected to determine whether they are appropriate for my research.

☐ I have familiarized myself with the ABCs of evaluation.

☐ I have evaluated the sources I've collected to date.

☐ I have taken notes to summarize, paraphrase, and directly quote my sources—and to record my own ideas.

☐ I understand the principle of plagiarism, have investigated my school's policy on plagiarism, and know how to prevent plagiarism or allegations of it.

☐ I have recorded the bibliographic data of the sources I will use in my research assignment.

☐ I know which citation style to use for my research assignment and have consulted the corresponding style guide.

☐ I have saved my work and backed it up appropriately.

☐ I have reflected on the research process, where I am in the process, and what steps I need to take next.

Taking Notes

Legend: Q – Quote   P – Paraphrase   ME – My insights

Citation:

Call number: ☐ Academic Library   ☐ Online

☐ Public Library   ☐ Other

Q

P

ME

Bibliographic Data Tracker

GRAB & GO

Book

1. Author(s) _____

2. Title & subtitle _____

3. Edition _____

4. Location of publication _____

5. Name of publisher _____

6. Year of publication _____

Internet Source

1. Author(s) _____

2. Document title _____

3. Title of database/website/periodical from which the document was accessed

    _____

4. Date of electronic publication or last update _____

5. Name of sponsoring institution/organization associated with the site

    _____

6. Date source was accessed _____

7. URL (Web address) _____

Bibliographic Data Tracker

GRAB & GO

Article in a Scholarly Journal

1. Author(s) _____

2. Article title_____

3. Journal title _____

4. Volume and/or issue number_____

5. Date of publication_____

6. Page number of the article_____

Newspaper or Magazine Article

1. Author(s) _____

2. Article title_____

3. Name of periodical _____

4. Publication date _____

5. Page number of the article_____

Getting It Out There: Communicating Your Research

After the evaluation phase of the research process comes the creation phase. Here's where the magic happens. Now is the time to develop how you will communicate the results of your research. In the case of a research paper, that means you need to write your thesis statement, outline or structure your paper, and get drafting.

Beyond the Research Paper: Killer Presentation, Anyone?

Earlier you considered the requirements of your research assignment. If you have some format options available, you might want to ask yourself if an essay really is the best option for communicating your research. Why not consider other ways of getting your research out there—for example, with a presentation? You'll find some helpful tips on putting together a killer PowerPoint presentation later on in this section (page 110). And here are some additional options for presenting your research results:

(Continued)

99

- **Visual:** research poster, display, website, video clip, Prezi presentation (page 112), spreadsheet
- **Oral:** interview, panel discussion, debate, seminar, podcast, teleconference
- **Written:** article, review, newsletter, media release, blog

A Note on Inspiration: Thesis Time!

Now that you've done the research, it's time to identify your thesis. So what exactly is a thesis, anyway? Simply put, a thesis is the *focus of a piece of writing*. Your thesis statement is a guide for your reader, telling him or her what exactly you'll be arguing in your paper.

What precedes the crafting of a good thesis statement is a moment of inspiration or insight—a lightbulb moment, if you will. Insight, however, doesn't happen overnight; it develops gradually over a period of time. Although you can't force insight or inspiration, you *can* plan for it. Give yourself enough time in the research process to let your ideas percolate and develop organically. Build in reflective time for yourself, including time for

- brainstorming again
- arranging and rearranging your research notes
- tweaking your research focus to better reflect the knowledge you've gained from the new sources you've encountered

We Can't Forget about Bloom!

Understood through the framework of Bloom's Taxonomy, a thesis statement highlights your synthesis of the information to create something new. It introduces your viewpoint or argument, a unique construction built upon the development of your ideas.

The End Is in Sight: Constructing a Thesis Statement

Different disciplines have their own particular ways of forming thesis statements. It's important to check in with your professor, instructor, TA, teacher, etc., at this stage of the game to make sure your thesis statement conforms to his or her expectations.

Despite the differences among disciplines, here are some generalizations about persuasive writing and crafting a good thesis statement. A good thesis statement is

- a clearly stated position that focuses on one main idea
- an assertion capable of being supported by your research
- a statement that indicates the result of your research and informs your reader about where the research paper is headed
- as a result of the point above, kind of a spoiler!

There are great resources to help you craft a strong thesis statement. Some of these include

- academic library websites
- college and university writing centers
- your local librarian
- resources listed in the sidebar Recommended Books on Writing and Research
- the template Crafting a Thesis Statement (Grab & Go page 115)

Don't be shy. Part of being a research virtuoso is having the courage and initiative to seek assistance. And, here's a sample approach to crafting a thesis:

Crafting a Thesis Statement

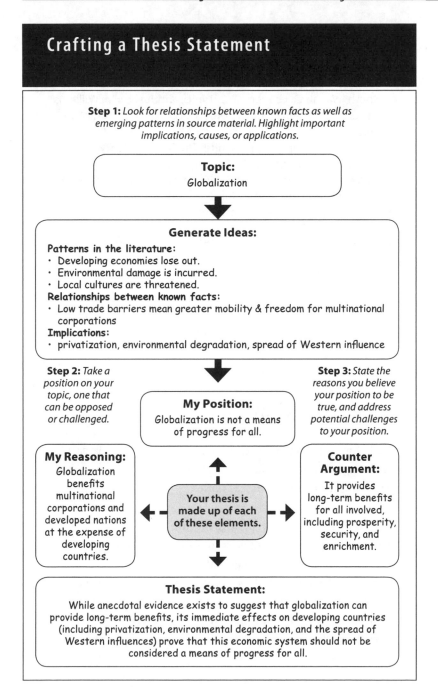

Step 1: *Look for relationships between known facts as well as emerging patterns in source material. Highlight important implications, causes, or applications.*

Topic:
Globalization

Generate Ideas:

Patterns in the literature:
- Developing economies lose out.
- Environmental damage is incurred.
- Local cultures are threatened.

Relationships between known facts:
- Low trade barriers mean greater mobility & freedom for multinational corporations

Implications:
- privatization, environmental degradation, spread of Western influence

Step 2: *Take a position on your topic, one that can be opposed or challenged.*

My Position:
Globalization is not a means of progress for all.

Step 3: *State the reasons you believe your position to be true, and address potential challenges to your position.*

My Reasoning:
Globalization benefits multinational corporations and developed nations at the expense of developing countries.

Your thesis is made up of each of these elements.

Counter Argument:
It provides long-term benefits for all involved, including prosperity, security, and enrichment.

Thesis Statement:
While anecdotal evidence exists to suggest that globalization can provide long-term benefits, its immediate effects on developing countries (including privatization, environmental degradation, and the spread of Western influences) prove that this economic system should not be considered a means of progress for all.

Recommended Books on Writing and Research

- Booth, Wayne C., Gregory G. Colomb, and Joseph M. Williams. *The Craft of Research*. 3rd ed. Chicago: University of Chicago Press, 2008.
- Strunk, William Jr., and E.B. White. *The Elements of Style*. 4th ed. New York, Longman, 2003.
- *MLA Handbook for Writers of Research Papers*. 7th ed. New York: Modern Language Association of America, 2009.
- Soles, Derek. *The Essentials of Academic Writing*. 2nd ed. Boston: Wadsworth, 2010.
- Northey, Margot, and Joan McKibbin. *Making Sense: A Student's Guide to Research and Writing*. 6th ed. Don Mills, ON: Oxford University Press, 2009.

Looking at Structure

How will you organize your information and ideas? Look carefully at your assignment for guidance. Here are some possible ways to structure research papers and examples:

- **chronologically**—past, present, future
- **sequentially**—first point, second point, third point
- **micro to macro**—local to global
- **macro to micro**—the global economic system to a specific market
- **compare and contrast**—similar versus different; positive versus negative

Try mapping out your ideas using sticky notes again (page 83). Alternatively, if you are writing a compare and contrast paper, you might want to use a Venn diagram to help structure your writing. See page 13 and Grab & Go page 27.

A Note on Perspiration

Genius is one percent inspiration, ninety-nine percent perspiration.
Thomas Edison, 1847–1931

Research is hard work. Being a research virtuoso is sort of like being a detective: you have to find information from different places, use analytical skills to evaluate the information, and eventually decide how the pieces fit together. Communicating your results by finishing a research paper is like solving a case—it's a challenge, but when it's done the final product is extremely rewarding.

Putting It All Together: The Anatomy of a Great Paper

What is essential to any good research paper? Here's a list:

- The paper should be original.
- It should be well researched.
- It should satisfy the expectations of the assignment.
- Its thesis statement should be supported by strong points in the body of the essay.

- It should explore divergent points of view and substantiate why you chose certain viewpoints over others.
- It should be cited appropriately and carefully—in other words, it must avoid plagiarism or accusations of plagiarism.
- It should include a well-formatted bibliography or works cited list.
- It should be something that you are proud to put your name on and you are proud to hand in.

Another mark of a good research paper is that you can talk about the salient points of your argument without having to refer to what you have written or any notes.

A Look at Process: Plan for Breaks!

In an ideal situation, you should finish your research and then take at least a day's break before starting to draft your paper. Then you should take a break after drafting and before revising, and another break before doing a final edit. This will allow you to look at the draft with a fresh set of eyes. And if you find you need to swing back to an earlier stage in the research process—to dig up more sources, follow a footnote, check a quote, or even tweak your research focus—the extra time will come in handy!

Sometimes someone else's eyes are even better than your own! If you have time, visit your university or college's writing center and make an appointment with one of its volunteer editors. This step is well worth it, but it does assume that you've left yourself quite a bit of time before the deadline. If you're running a little low on time, why not ask a friend or family member to look over your draft?

Title Hunting

On the hunt for a good title? If not, consider it! Remember, it's the first thing that your professor sees, setting the tone for what's to come. Here are some tips for writing a good title:

1. **Write it last:** Some people consider the title the *pièce de résistance* of a research paper—the best part, the showpiece. It's a good idea to leave its creation to the very end, when you have a sense of the bigger picture.

2. **Incorporate key terms and concepts:** When you have a clear, concise title that reflects your paper's content with key terms and concepts, it indicates a cohesive, focused paper. Your reader will be left with a sense of unity. And (we hope) you will be left with a better mark!

3. **Subheadings are your friend:** Remember the point above? We sure hope so because you just read it. Two-part titles give you more room for key terms, so use them!

The Grand Finale: A Checklist

For the final touches to your masterpiece, follow this five-point checklist:

1. EVALUATE YOUR CONTENT

a) Before you go any further with your draft, make sure you have met the requirements of the assignment. Ask yourself:

- Have I fully and clearly addressed all aspects of the assignment?
- If there was room for creativity, have I made good use of that option?

b) Is there anything you need to change about the content?

- Have you found new information to incorporate?
- Does your draft still contain old information that shouldn't be there and needs to be deleted?
- Has your understanding of the topic changed? Do you need to revise your thesis to reflect this?

c) Read your draft out loud. Although it might frighten your housemates, this technique can have a big impact on the final product. Reading out loud brings unclear expression and simple errors to your attention—for example, a missing word. If you feel too silly reading to yourself, ask someone else to do it while you listen.

2. VERIFY THE FACTS

When you're rushed or trying to make sense of information, you're vulnerable to jotting down facts incorrectly. Now's the time to check and change! Go back to your sources and verify key facts and details such as the following:

- spelling of names
- wording of quotations
- statistics
- dates

3. CHECK TRANSITIONS, LANGUAGE, AND MECHANICS

Double-check your draft line by line and word by word. Do a last reading for mechanical errors in spelling, grammar, and punctuation.

- Have you written transitional sentences to help connect the ideas in the paper? If not, now's the time!
- Consider the particular words and phrases you've used. Can you alter your choices in language for clarity and emphasis? Is there a more appropriate phrase you should use?
- Although handy, your computer's spell-check can be your undoing; it doesn't catch mistakes like the difference between *your* and *you're*. What grammar errors can you spot? On the importance of punctuation, check out books such as *Eats, Shoots & Leaves*, by Lynne Truss.

4. POLISH YOUR DOCUMENTATION

Make sure you have properly cited all the information you've gathered from other sources.

- Have you used the style your professor, instructor, teacher, etc., specified?

- Have you used that style correctly?
- Are all your in-text citations accurate?
- Is your works cited list complete and accurate?

5. THINK ABOUT PRESENTATION

To make your research findings truly presentable, consider the following:

- Does your cover page clearly state the title of the assignment? Does it conform to the required style guideline?
- Make sure your instructor's name is spelled correctly when submitting your paper or presentation!
- Have you double-spaced your text and numbered all the pages?
- Have you inserted all the pictures, graphs, and diagrams you planned to include?

Bucking the Trend: Submitting a Presentation

Beyond the research paper, presentations are one of the most popular ways for researchers to get their findings and ideas across. Just like a research paper, a presentation should be well researched, well organized, and properly introduced.

If you put together a multimedia slideshow (e.g., a PowerPoint presentation) to communicate your research, here are some points to consider:

INTRODUCTION

Begin a slideshow presentation with an introduction or title page that lists

- the title of your presentation
- the purpose of the presentation—e.g., is it for a particular class?
- the name of the presenter—that's you!
- the date of the presentation

BODY

- Plan to *present* your presentation rather than read it word for word from the slides. After all, your audience can read the slides for themselves.
- Write in point form or short sentences. You can expand on each point verbally. A whole whack of text is, well, just plain boring.
- Consider memorizing key statements; if you can look your audience in the eye when presenting this information, they'll be impressed.
- Choose your fonts carefully. Pick ones that can be read easily and are appropriate to the tone of your presentation.
- Include images and multimedia, such as video or audio files. Check that these *enhance* the text and *support* the main ideas of the presentation—in other words, they shouldn't just be great visuals to liven things up.
- Have a back-up plan just in case something goes wrong in your presentation. Preload any web pages or clips you want to link to. Sure, it's flashier to click a link in a presentation and go automatically to a website or video clip or audio clip, but having preloaded content to open manually will save you if the links don't work in front of your audience.

CONCLUSION

Summarize your main points. Include a list of sources used to compile the information for the presentation. Generally, a works cited list should be the last slide of your presentation.

Presentation Software

Do you want to impress your peers and your professor or instructor with your presentation savvy? Consider using an online-presentation application when putting together a presentation. Both choices below have free and paid options.

- **Prezi:** a zooming presentation editor that allows you to zoom in and out to see the big picture as well as the details
- **SlideRocket:** presentation software that lets you input existing presentations and upload online photos and videos with ease; also has the capability for real-time feeds online

Standing on the Shoulders of Giants

If I have seen farther it is by standing on the shoulders of giants.

Isaac Newton, 1642–1727

Believe it or not, not that much has changed in the world of research over the last three centuries. Sure, we have better tools at our disposal—namely the Internet—but searching for, evaluating, sorting, crediting, and building on information remain the primary pursuits of all researchers.

It is the research virtuoso's privilege to add to what we know in the world. Although infused with your own creativity and insight, your completed research will most likely interpret and build on the work of others. Maybe one day your own work will help to inspire budding research virtuosos, thus contributing to the ancient cycle of give and take that makes up the academic world.

Looking Back

Congratulations on making it through the research process! At this stage of the game, a research virtuoso reflects on what he or she has learned along the way.

- Which stages of research did you find the most challenging? Why?
- What have you learned about the research process that you didn't already know?
- Have you acquired any new skills along the way? If so, how do you envision using them in the future?
- Are there ways in which you could have improved the final product? Don't forget to ask your professor (or instructor, etc.) for his or her opinion on the matter; office hours are a perfect time to do just that.

Get Organized Checklist:
Getting It Out There

GRAB & GO

- ☐ I have met all assignment requirements.

- ☐ If choosing an alternative format is an option, I have considered the most appropriate way to present my research, including visual, oral, or written methods.

- ☐ I have consulted authoritative sources on crafting my writing, including developing a persuasive thesis statement.

- ☐ I have completed the five-point checklist (pages 107–110) to evaluate the content of my draft; verify the facts; check my transitions, language, and mechanics; polish my documentation; and think about my presentation.

- ☐ I have come up with a thoughtful title.

- ☐ I have reflected on the research process, what I've learned, and how I can improve.

Crafting a Thesis Statement

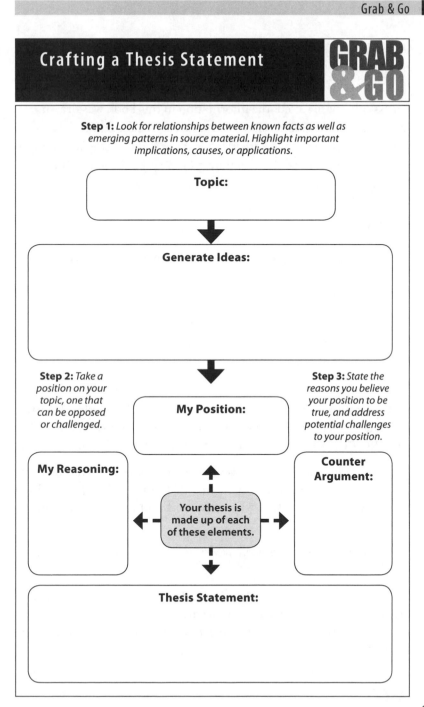

Step 1: *Look for relationships between known facts as well as emerging patterns in source material. Highlight important implications, causes, or applications.*

Topic:

Generate Ideas:

Step 2: *Take a position on your topic, one that can be opposed or challenged.*

My Position:

Step 3: *State the reasons you believe your position to be true, and address potential challenges to your position.*

My Reasoning:

Counter Argument:

Your thesis is made up of each of these elements.

Thesis Statement:

Works Cited
|||||||||||||||||||||||||||||||||||||||||||||||

Unless otherwise stated, the information in this book was drawn from the Toronto Public Library's resources, including the first edition of this book (*The Research Virtuoso: Brilliant Methods for Normal Brains*, by the Toronto Public Library, published in 2006 by Annick Press).

SECTION 1

"Audience." The Writing Center. University of North Carolina at Chapel Hill. 2007. Accessed online April 21, 2011. http://www.unc.edu/depts/wcweb/handouts/audience.html

Bolden, Tonya. *George Washington Carver.* New York: Abrams Books for Young Readers, 2009.

Booth, Wayne C., Gregory G. Colomb, and Joseph M. Williams. *The Craft of Research.* 3rd ed. Chicago: University of Chicago Press, 2008.

Coffey, Heather. "Bloom's Taxonomy." LEARN NC. University of North Carolina at Chapel Hill School of Education. 2008. Accessed online April 19, 2011. http://www.learnnc.org/lp/pages/4719?ref=search

"The Data Deluge: Businesses, Governments and Society Are Only Starting to Tap Its Vast Potential." *The Economist.* 25 February 2010. Accessed online August 2, 2011. http://www.economist.com/node/15579717?story_id=15579717

Greene, Carol. *George Washington Carver: Scientist and Teacher.* Chicago: Childrens Press, 1992.

"How to Channel the Data Deluge in Academic Research." *The Chronicle of Higher Education.* April 4, 2008. Academic OneFile. Online database accessed August 2, 2011. http://chronicle.com/article/How-to-Channel-the-Data-Deluge/17878

Imagine the Learning @ Your Library. Toronto: Toronto District School Board, 2006.

McLuhan, Marshall. *Understanding Media: The Extensions of Man.* Critical edition. Edited by W. Terrence Gordon. Corte Madera, CA: Gingko Press, 2003.

Reeve, Roger M., Cadance A. Lowell, Darren H. Touchell, Christina Walters, and Eric E. Roos. "Seed." AccessScience. 2008. McGraw-Hill. Online database accessed August 2, 2011.

Research Success @ Your Library: A Guide for Secondary Students. Toronto: Toronto District School Board, 2005.

Think Literacy: Library Research, Grades 7–12. Toronto: Ontario School Library Association, 2005.

Toronto Public Library (text), Joe Weissmann (art). *The Research Virtuoso: Brilliant Methods for Normal Brains.* Toronto: Annick Press, 2006.

"Understanding Assignments." The Writing Center. University of North Carolina at Chapel Hill. 2007. Accessed online August 2, 2011. http://www.unc.edu/depts/wcweb/handouts/readassign.html

SECTION 2

Booth, Wayne C., et al. *The Craft of Research.* (See Works Cited—Section 1.)

Caseñas, Carolyn, and Katherine Kalsbeek. "Archival Research Tutorial." York University Libraries, Clara Thomas Archives and Special Collections. 2006. Accessed online April 25, 2011. http://www.library.yorku.ca/binaries/ArchivesSpecialCollections/Guides_York/index.html

"Effective Online Searching Strategies" in *Research Success @ Your Library.* (See Works Cited—Section 1.)

Imagine the Learning @ Your Library. (See Works Cited—Section 1.)

Parks, Rosa, and James Haskins. *Rosa Parks: My Story.* New York: Dial Books, 1992.

Pearce-Moses, Richard. "Archival Records." *A Glossary of Archival and Records Terminology.* The Society of American Archivists. 2005. Accessed online May 6, 2011. http://www.archivists.org/glossary/term_details.asp?DefinitionKey=292

Toronto Public Library. *The Research Virtuoso.* (See Works Cited—Section 1.)

SECTION 3

Bell, Suzanne S. *Librarian's Guide to Online Searching.* Westport, CT: Libraries Unlimited, 2006.

Booth, Wayne C., et al. *The Craft of Research.* (See Works Cited—Section 1.)

"Cloud Computing." *Encyclopædia Britannica. Encyclopædia Britannica Online Library Edition.* Encyclopædia Britannica, 2011. Online database accessed May 18, 2011. http://library.eb.com/eb/article-9474374

"Editors' Note." *The New York Times.* December 2, 2005. Accessed online August 2, 2011. http://query.nytimes.com/gst/fullpage.html?res=990CE0 D61531F931A35751C1A9639C8B63

George, Mary W. *The Elements of Library Research: What Every Student Needs to Know.* Princeton, NJ: Princeton University Press, 2008.

Godin, Seth. "The Future of the Library." Seth Godin's Blog. May 16, 2011. Accessed online June 2, 2011. http://sethgodin.typepad.com/seths_blog/2011/05/the-future-of-the-library.html

Lewis, Norman P. "Plagiarism Antecedents and Situational Influences." *Journalism and Mass Communication Quarterly* 85, no. 2 (Summer 2008): 313–330. Accessed online August 2, 2011. http://www.aejmc.org/_scholarship/research_use/jmcq/08sum/lewis_text.pdf

McLuhan, Marshall. *Understanding Media.* (See Works Cited—Section 1.)

Peet, Richard. *Unholy Trinity: The IMF, World Bank, and WTO.* London: Zed Books, 2003.

"Pranksters Are Altering Entries on Wikipedia; The Whip." *The Sun* [London, England] February 13, 2006: 24. InfoTrac Newsstand. Online database accessed August 2, 2011.

Research Success @ Your Library. (See Works Cited—Section 1.)

Sawers, Neil. *Ten Steps to Help You Write Better Essays & Term Papers: I Wish I'd Had This When I Was in School!* Edmonton: NS Group, 2002.

Stolley, Karl, and Allen Brizee. "Safe Practices." Purdue Online Writing Lab. April 21, 2010. Accessed online June 30, 2011. http://owl.english. purdue.edu/owl/resource/589/03/

Toronto Public Library. *The Research Virtuoso.* (See Works Cited— Section 1.)

SECTION 4

Booth, Wayne C., et al. *The Craft of Research.* (See Works Cited—Section 1.)

Darity, William A., Jr., ed. *International Encyclopedia of the Social Sciences.* Vol. 5. 2nd ed. Detroit: Macmillan Reference USA, 2008: 102–103.

Lambrick, Melanie. "Counterpoint: Globalization Benefits Powerful Businesses at the Expense of Poor Nations." *Canadian Points of View: Globalization.* 2009. Online database accessed June 16, 2011.

"Newton, Isaac." *Complete Dictionary of Scientific Biography* 10. Detroit: Charles Scribner's Sons, 2008 : 42–101. Gale Virtual Reference Library. Online database accessed June 16, 2011.

Newton, Isaac. "Standing on the Shoulders of Giants." The Phrase Finder. Accessed online August 5, 2011. http://www.phrases.org.uk/ meanings/268025.html

Research Success @ Your Library. (See Works Cited—Section 1.)

Toronto Public Library. *The Research Virtuoso.* (See Works Cited— Section 1.)

Index